Everyman, I will go with thee,
and be thy guide

THE EVERYMAN
LIBRARY

The Everyman Library was founded by J. M. Dent
in 1906. He chose the name Everyman because he wanted
to make available the best books ever written in every
field to the greatest number of people at the cheapest possible
price. He began with Boswell's 'Life of Johnson';
his one-thousandth title was Aristotle's 'Metaphysics',
by which time sales exceeded forty million.

Today Everyman paperbacks remain true to
J. M. Dent's aims and high standards, with a wide range
of titles at affordable prices in editions which address
the needs of today's readers. Each new text is reset to give
a clear, elegant page and to incorporate the latest thinking
and scholarship. Each book carries the pilgrim logo,
the character in 'Everyman', a medieval morality play,
a proud link between Everyman
past and present.

Thomas Hardy

SELECTED POEMS

Edited by
ANDREW MOTION

EVERYMAN
J. M. DENT · LONDON
CHARLES E. TUTTLE
VERMONT

Introduction, chronology and other critical apparatus
© J. M. Dent 1994

This edition first published in Everyman by J. M. Dent in 1994
Reprinted 1997

J. M. Dent
Orion Publishing Group
Orion House, 5 Upper St Martin's Lane,
London WC2H 9EA
and
Charles E. Tuttle Co. Inc.
28 South Main Street,
Rutland, Vermont 05701, USA

Typeset in Sabon by CentraCet Ltd, Linton, Cambridge
Printed in Great Britain by
The Guernsey Press Co. Ltd, Guernsey, C.I.

British Library Cataloguing-in-Publication Data
is available upon request.

ISBN 0 460 87458 6

CONTENTS

from TIME'S LAUGHINGSTOCKS AND OTHER VERSES

NOTE ON THE AUTHOR AND EDITOR

THOMAS HARDY was born on 2 June 1840 in Higher Bockhampton near Dorchester, the son of a stonemason and builder, and a former domestic servant, Jemima Hand. After an education that included Latin, French and mathematics, Hardy was articled at sixteen to a Dorchester architect and in 1862 went to work in London. He pursued a programme of self-education with a view to entering the church, but by 1863 was already considering becoming a writer. He returned to Dorset in 1867 and began his first (unpublished) novel, *The Poor Man and the Lady*. In 1870 he went to St Juliot in Cornwall to survey the church and met Emma Lavinia Gifford, the rector's sister-in-law. The publication of *Desperate Remedies* (1871), *Under the Greenwood Tree* (1872) and *A Pair of Blue Eyes* (serialized from September 1872) encouraged Hardy to give up architecture for writing, and the success of *Far from the Madding Crowd* in 1874 enabled him to marry Emma.

After a number of moves between London and Dorset, the Hardys finally settled in 1885 at Max Gate near Dorchester, where Hardy continued to write novels and short stories, but the harsh reviews of *Jude the Obscure* (1895) encouraged him to relinquish fiction for poetry. *Wessex Poems* appeared in 1898. Although their marriage was unhappy, Emma inspired some of Hardy's most memorable verse, written after her death in 1912. He married Florence Emily Dugdale in 1914. By Hardy's death in 1928 he had written over 900 poems, and had also published a vast epic drama, *The Dynasts*. He was awarded the Order of Merit in 1910.

ANDREW MOTION is a poet and biographer. His most recent publications are *Philip Larkin: A Writer's Life* (Faber, 1993), and *The Price of Everything* (Faber, 1994).

CHRONOLOGY OF HARDY'S LIFE

CHRONOLOGY OF HIS TIMES

Year	Literary Context	Historical Events
1840		Great Irish famine
		Penny Post introduced
1842		Chartist riots
1846		Repeal of Corn Laws
1847	Charlotte Brontë, *Jane Eyre*	Railway reaches Dorchester
	Emily Brontë, *Wuthering Heights*	
1848	Dickens, *Dombey and Son*	
	Thackeray, *Vanity Fair*	
	Pre-Raphaelite Brotherhood active	
1849	Ruskin, *Seven Lamps of Architecture*	
1850	Death of Wordsworth	
	Tennyson becomes Poet Laureate	
1851		The Great Exhibition in London
1853	Arnold, *Poems*	1853–6 The Crimean War
1855	Browning, *Men and Women*	
	Elizabeth Gaskell, *North and South*	
1858	George Eliot, *Scenes of Clerical Life*	
1859	Darwin, *On the Origin of Species*	
1860	Wilkie Collins, *The Woman in White*	
1861	Palgrave's anthology, *The Golden Treasury*	American Civil War
	Hymns Ancient and Modern	

Year	Age	Life
1860s		Throughout this decade Hardy steadily loses his religious faith
1865	25	A short fictional piece called 'How I Built Myself a House' published
1867	27	Returns to Dorset, begins his first novel, *The Poor Man and the Lady*
1868	28	Romantic affair with his cousin, Tryphena Sparks. *The Poor Man and the Lady* rejected by publishers
1869	29	Works in Weymouth for an architect
1870	30	Meets and falls in love with Emma Lavinia Gifford while at St Juliot in Cornwall planning the restoration of the church
1871	31	*Desperate Remedies*, published anonymously, is a commercial failure
1872	32	Has minor success with *Under the Greenwood Tree*
1873	33	*A Pair of Blue Eyes*, Hardy's first novel to appear as a serial. Becomes a full-time novelist
1874	34	*Far from the Madding Crowd*, his first real success. Marries Emma Gifford. For next nine years they move from one lodging to another
1878	38	*The Return of the Native*. Becomes member of London's Savile Club
1879	39	His short story 'The Distracted Preacher' published
1880	40	*The Trumpet-Major*. Is taken ill for several months
1881	41	*A Laodicean*
1882	42	*Two on a Tower*. Visits Paris
1885	45	Moves into Max Gate, house on outskirts of Dorchester. Lives there for the rest of his life
1886	46	*The Mayor of Casterbridge*. Sees Impressionist paintings in London

Year	Literary Context	Historical Events
1863	Death of Thackeray Mill, *Utilitarianism*	
1864	Newman, *Apologia pro Vita Sua*	
1865	Death of Elizabeth Gaskell	
1866	Swinburne, *Poems and Ballads*	
1867	Ibsen, *Peer Gynt*	Second Reform Bill
1868		Gladstone becomes Prime Minister
1869	Mill, *The Subjection of Women*	
1870	Death of Dickens	Franco-Prussian War Education Act brings education for all
1871	Darwin, *The Descent of Man*	Trade Unions legalized
1874		Disraeli becomes Prime Minister The modern bicycle arrives
1876	Henry James's novels begin to be published	
1878		Edison invents the incandescent electric lamp
1879	James Murray becomes editor of what was later to become *The Oxford English Dictionary* Ibsen, *A Doll's House*	
1880	Death of George Eliot Zola, *Nana*	
1881	Revised Version of New Testament	Married Woman's Property Act
1882	Deaths of Darwin, D. G. Rossetti and Trollope	Daimler's petrol engine
1885	Birth of D. H. Lawrence	Salisbury becomes Prime Minister
1886	Death of William Barnes, friend of Hardy, poet, philologist, polymath	

Year	Literary Context	Historical Events
1887	Strindberg, *The Father*	
1888	Death of Arnold Birth of T. S. Eliot About now the work of Kipling and Yeats begin to be published	
1889	Deaths of Browning, Hopkins and Wilkie Collins	
1890	Death of Newman	First underground railway in London
1891	Shaw, *Quintessence of Ibsenism*	
1892	Death of Tennyson	Gladstone Prime Minister
1893	Pinero, *The Second Mrs Tanqueray*	Independent Labour Party set up
1894	Deaths of Stevenson and Pater	Rosebery becomes Prime Minister
1895	Conrad's first novel, *Almayer's Folly* published Wilde, *The Importance of Being Earnest*	Salisbury becomes Prime Minister Freud's first work on psycho-analysis Marconi's 'wireless' telegraphy
1896	Housman, *A Shropshire Lad*	
1898	Wells, *The War of the Worlds*	The Curies discover radium
1899		The Boer War begins
1900	Deaths of Ruskin and Wilde	
1901		Death of Queen Victoria; succeeded by Edward VII
1902	Death of Zola; Hardy laments his death	Balfour becomes Prime Minister
1903		Wright brothers make first flight in aeroplane with engine
1904	Chekhov, *The Cherry Orchard*	
1906		Liberals win election
1907	Kipling awarded Nobel Prize	
1908		Asquith becomes Prime Minister

Year	Age	Life
1909	69	*Time's Laughingstocks* (94 poems)
1910	70	Awarded the Order of Merit
1911	71	Ceases spending 'the season' in London
1912	72	Death of his wife, Emma. The Wessex Edition of his works published by Macmillan
1913	73	*A Changed Man and Other Tales.* Revisits Cornwall and the scenes of his courtship of Emma
1914	74	*Satires of Circumstance* (107 poems). Marries Florence Emily Dugdale
1915	75	Death of his sister, Mary
1916	76	*Selected Poems of Thomas Hardy* edited by Hardy himself
1917	77	*Moments of Vision* (159 poems). Begins to write his autobiography with intention that Florence should publish it under her own name after his death
1919–20	79	A de-luxe edition of his work, the Mellstock Edition, published
1920 onwards	80	Max Gate becomes a place of pilgrimage for hundreds of admirers
1922	82	*Late Lyrics and Earlier* (151 poems)
1923	83	*The Queen of Cornwall* (a poetic play)
1924	84	Hardy's adaptation of *Tess* performed in Dorchester
1925	85	*Human Shows* (152 poems)

Year	Literary Context	Historical Events
1909	Deaths of Swinburne and Meredith	
1910		Death of Edward VII; succeeded by George V
1911	Bennett, *Clayhanger* Brooke, *Poems*	
1912		Sinking of *Titanic*
1913	D. H. Lawrence, *Sons and Lovers*	First Morris Oxford car
1914	Pound edits the first anthology of Imagist poetry Frost, *North of Boston*	The First World War begins
1915	Woolf, *The Voyage Out*	
1916	Death of James D. H. Lawrence's *The Rainbow* seized by police	Lloyd George becomes Prime Minister The Russian Revolution
1918	Siegfried Sassoon, *Counter-Attack* Hopkins, *Poems*	The war ends Women over thirty given the vote
1919		Treaty of Versailles First woman MP
1920	Edward Thomas, *Collected Poems* Wilfred Owen, *Poems*	First meeting of League of Nations
1922	T. S. Eliot, *The Waste Land* Joyce, *Ulysses*	Mussolini comes to power Women given equality in divorce proceedings
1924	Forster, *A Passage to India*	Ramsay MacDonald forms first Labour Government Stalin becomes Soviet Dictator
1926	T. E. Lawrence, *Seven Pillars of Wisdom*	The General Strike
1927		Lindbergh makes first crossing by air of the Atlantic

Year	Age	Life
1928	87	Hardy dies on 11 January; heart buried in Westminster Abbey, ashes in the family church at Stinsford. *Winter Words* (105 poems) is published posthumously. *The Early Life of Thomas Hardy*, his disguised autobiography, published
1930		*The Later Years of Thomas Hardy*, the second volume of the autobiography, published. *Collected Poems* (918 poems) followed by *The Complete Poems* (947 poems) in 1976
1937		Death of Hardy's second wife, Florence

Year	Literary Context	Historical Events
1928	D. H. Lawrence's *Lady Chatterley's Lover* privately printed in Florence	

INTRODUCTION

Hardy's life as a poet was extraordinarily long. His earliest known poem is 'Domicilium', written while he was still a teenager in the late 1850s. Forty-odd poems survive from the 1860s, but when he abandoned his career as an architect in the 1870s and began to write novels full-time, his poetry seems to have dried up. When he turned away from novels during the 1890s, his poems returned – in a flood which continued unabated until his death in 1928 at the age of eighty-seven.

Hardy's first biography – which was written by his second wife Florence but largely dictated by Hardy himself – raises the question of whether he switched from prose to poetry because his later novels were so fiercely criticized. It puts on a brave front:

> The misrepresentations of the last two or three years affected but little, if at all, the informed appreciation of Hardy's writings, being heeded almost entirely by those who had not read him; and turned out ultimately to be the best thing that could have happened; for they well-nigh compelled him, in his own judgement at any rate, if he wished to retain any shadow of self-respect, to abandon at once a form of literary art he had long intended to abandon at some indefinite time, and resume openly that form of it which had always been more instinctive with him, and which he had just been able to keep alive from his early years, half in secrecy, under the pressure of magazine writing.

Like much else in the biography, this is simultaneously assertive and coy. It lets us see that Hardy was hurt by criticism of his novels, even while denying it. It also hints at (but does not reveal) other motives, the most complicated of which were to do with the circumstances of his private life in general, and the difficulties of his marriage in particular. This persuaded him that his deepest feelings might find a more satisfactory release in the codifiable stanzas of a lyric poem than in the more expansive realms of prose.

Many of the critics who condemned Hardy's later fiction also attacked his poetry. Hardy, with steadily mounting impatience, insisted that his final vocation had always been his true one – not just for personal reasons, but because it allowed him to express what he called 'ideas and emotions which run counter to the inert crystallized opinion – hard as a rock – which the vast body of men have vested interests in supporting'. What he meant, plainly, was that he felt poems might allow him to continue with impunity the war on received opinion that he had waged at such cost in his novels – the war in which his allies were the great Victorian scientists and doubters Darwin, Lyell and Huxley. 'If Galileo had said in verse that the world moved', Hardy wrote wistfully, 'the Inquisition might have let him alone.'

But poems did not bring Hardy the quiet life that he envisaged. Critics who mocked him at the beginning of his new career turned out to be the forerunners of others who, for the next half-century and more, also disputed his merits by calling him uneven, occasional, narrow. In due course, the debate about his work became part of a larger argument between the Modernists and what we now know as 'the English Line'. Hardy, along with the Georgians, Edward Thomas and later poets like Philip Larkin, were interpreted as representatives of the poetic 'right', while Eliot, Pound and other technical radicals were associated with the 'left'.

Today such rigid distinctions have softened and Hardy the poet has begun to receive the kind of serious critical attention which had formerly been reserved for the difficult Modernists. Yet even his most enthusiastic admirers still respond to the enormous bulk of his *Collected Poems* with something like alarm. They are daunted not just by the volume of his work but by its diversity, rightly supposing that this forms a large part of its pleasure, and of its meaning.

As he pioneered the revival of Hardy's poetic fortunes in the 1960s, Philip Larkin certainly felt this. 'One can read him for years and years', he said, 'and still be surprised.' Other critics took the hint. How could anyone make an adequate selection from Hardy's work, they wanted to know, when no one agreed which were his best poems? Donald Davie, in *Thomas Hardy and British Poetry* (1973), appraised the received opinions. He rehearsed Larkin's views, added Mark Van Doren's opinion that 'no poet more stubbornly resists selection', and concluded: 'I for one find myself more and more of [their] way of thinking.' To solidify his doubt, he criticized a selection made by John Crowe Ransom in 1960, and then said: 'Cast about as one may, and measure one authority against another, one perceives no consensus emerging as to what is centrally significant in Hardy's poetry, still less therefore as to what is the canon of his secure achievements.'

For all Davie's sabre-rattling, his book is anxious to seem modest, in keeping with its hero. He says that what 'defeats the attempt to discriminate the better from the worse' is the fact that Hardy 'impresses himself on the reader hardly at all' and offers instead (in Hardy's own words) 'only a series of disconnected impressions'.

Five years later, in his tentatively titled but book-length *Essay*, John Bayley expanded these points. He argued that for Hardy the 'purity' of poetry 'consisted in not having to take the trouble to stimulate and display, to fashion surprises and strong conclusions'. Like Davie, he complimented Hardy for cultivating a deliberate unevenness, and for distributing 'cunning irregularities' of rhythm and tone throughout his work. His justification was a famous passage from Hardy's disguised autobiography:

> Years earlier [Hardy had written] he had decided that too regular a beat was bad art. He had fortified himself in his opinion by thinking of the analogy of architecture, between which art and that of poetry he had discovered, to use his own words, that there existed a close and curious parallel, both arts, unlike some others, having to carry a rational content inside their artistic form. He knew that in architecture cunning irregularity is of enormous worth, and it is obvious that he carried on into his verse, perhaps in part unconsciously, the Gothic art-principle in which he had been trained – the principle of spontaneity, found in the mouldings, tracery, and such like – resulting in the 'unforeseen' (as it has been called) character of his metres and stanzas, that of stress rather than syllable, poetic texture rather than poetic veneer.

Those who disparage Hardy say that his irregularities make him, whether he intends them or not, a hamfisted writer, someone in whose poems we find strengths and weaknesses lying uncomfortably closely together. Those who admire him say that his 'principle of spontaneity' is a sign of authenticity. This is certainly Davie's and Bayley's view, but their enthusiasm still is not strong enough to stop them doubting the value of a selection. Such a thing is impossible, Bayley says hesitantly, because of the poems' 'fictional skills and obfuscations'. More confidently, he announces that 'it does not really meet the case' to decide that the best poems are the autobiographical pieces 'written after the death of his first wife'.

Davie and Bayley want to have it both ways. On the one hand, they praise Hardy to the skies, and honour a tradition that runs parallel or counter to the Modernists. On the other, Davie says that Hardy's advocates have not 'yet found a way to make [him] *weigh* equally' with them. Once or twice, this gets Davie into a tight corner, especially when his moral sense rides piggy-back on his critical judgement. 'Are not Hardy and his successors right in severely curtailing for themselves the liberties that other poets take?' he asks at the end of his Introduction to *Thomas Hardy and British Poetry*. 'Does not the example of the Hardyesque poets make some of these other poets look childishly irresponsible?' The answer Davie expects to hear is evident everywhere in his book: he wants us to applaud – or at least to respect – Hardy's 'apparent meanness of spirit', his 'painful modesty of intention', his 'extremely limited objectives'.

Far from settling the question of what is best, this makes the whole issue even more complex. And there is something else, too. 'Hardy's poems', Davie says, form 'a body of writing before which one honest critic after another has by his own confession retired, baffled and defeated'. They have been bamboozled, he means to say, by the fact that regularities and irregularities, weaknesses and strengths, seem simultaneously to rely on each other and be careless of each other. Larkin acknowledges something of the same sort but does not mind it. If the commentators are 'baffled', he implies, no amount of 'honesty' will save their reputations: it merely proves that 'Hardy doesn't seem to attract the best modern critics'.

Why not? One reason is the poems' appearance of appropriating to themselves the job which is normally undertaken by a critic. For all their descriptions, their evocations, their flares and flashes of strong feeling, they often depend on arguments and interior dialogues which make the purpose of a poem not just to re-create something but to elucidate it. As they try to work their way through experience, they push critics to the sidelines.

The second kind of bafflement is different: it has to do with what we might loosely call pessimism. For those who think life is exactly as Hardy saw it – full of lost chances, shadowed by failure – there is no problem. For others, the prevailing mood of his poems is a limitation. Not surprisingly, people wishing to promote his reputation have tried to restrict the damage. One way is to insist, as Larkin himself does, that Hardy's pessimism is not a settled mood but the hallmark of an evolving person- ality. 'Hardy associated sensitivity to suffering and awareness of the causes of pain with superior spiritual character', he tells us. And again, *à propos* the novels: 'The presence of pain is a positive quality . . . [it is] the continual imaginative celebration of what is both the truest and most important element in life, most important in the sense of most necessary to spiritual development.'

Saying this, Larkin is remembering Hardy's Apology in *Late Lyrics and Earlier* (1922), where we find:

> What is . . . alleged to be 'pessimism' is, in truth, only such 'questionings' in the exploration of reality, and is the first step towards the soul's betterment, and the body's also. If I may be forgiven for quoting my own old words, let me repeat what I printed in this relation more than twenty years ago, and wrote much earlier, in a poem entitled 'In Tenebris':
>
> > If way to the Better there be, it exacts a full look at the Worst:
>
> that is to say, by the exploration of reality, and its frank recog- nition stage by stage along the survey, with an eye to the best consummation possible: briefly, evolutionary meliorism.

In its high-minded way, this passage wants us to believe that all Hardy's poems are engaged in a self-improving tussle. Many of them are, pitching love against disappointment, happiness against sorrow, hope against death. But there are also many other poems in which his pessimism seems to be of the crudest and most enveloping kind. In his lyric poems, it becomes an automatic negativity, something we find him trying to pass off as a joke in 'Epitaph on a Pessimist' but which he nevertheless often puts forward in all seriousness: 'I'm Smith of Stoke, aged sixty-odd,/I've lived without a dame/From youth-time on; and would to God/My dad had done the same.' In his ballads and story poems the same doggedness produces narrative inflexi- bility. A poem like 'The Rash Birds', for instance, shows Hardy

pretending to create a miniature drama, whereas in fact he is
playing a five-finger exercise on the theme of life's little ironies.
'A Sound in the Night', from *Late Lyrics and Earlier*, is another
example. The poem has a number of familiar Hardy ingredients
– bad weather, ghostly presences, social disjunction – and
describes a couple on their wedding night hearing a noise 'like
the crying of a woman' from outside the 'farmstead once a
castle' in which they are living. The husband goes to investigate,
returns wet and shaking, then reveals to his wife: 'There was one
I loved once: the cry you heard was her cry'. The poem ends:

> They found a woman's body at a spot called Rocky Shallow,
> Where the Froom stream curves amid the moorland, washed
>   aground,
> And they searched about for him, the yeoman, who had darkly
>   known her,
>   But he could not be found.
>
> And the bride left for good-and-all the farmstead once a castle,
> And in a county far away lives, mourns, and sleeps alone,
> And thinks in windy weather that she hears a woman crying,
>   And sometimes an infant's moan.

In spite of its rhythmical drive, its cunning irregularities, and
its well-managed conventions, this poem disappoints us. We
neither quail at the neo-Gothic ghoul nor do we recognize,
within and beyond it, a mature sceptical philosophy. Instead,
and especially when we read the poem among Hardy's many
other similar ones, we experience something unfeeling in its
gloom. Too often, Hardy welcomes mischance in his poems not
as a way of proving the sadness of existence, but of protecting
himself against its variety. He sometimes closes down his options
too quickly. He can be heartlessly word-perfect in his response
to sorrow.

Inevitably, this makes him sound complacent. More strangely,
it breeds the inappropriate kind of camp we hear in the
miniature workings of his language as well as his idiom generally. It is there, for example, in the knowing use of idiosyncratic
words and phrases for which he is renowned ('wonning',
'dissolubility', 'catering care', 'choric bent'). It is there, too, in
the notorious moments when his absolutism breaks cover and
takes definite forms: 'the vague Immense', 'the Great Fate', 'King
Doom', 'Willer', 'the all-immense Will', 'the phantom Ironic'.

Because they are so cartoon-like, these figures mock the ideas which are meant to inform them, ideas that are successfully handled in another, more restrained, poem, 'God's Funeral'. Whereas in some writers camp is a sign of gravity in Hardy it is a mark of incompetence.

Once again, Hardy's admirers routinely forgive him these things by referring to them as further aspects of his authenticity (the 'all is best' argument again). It might do Hardy's reputation more good if they were called clumsy and regarded as fault-lines between a nineteenth-century sensibility and a modern one, between an autodidactical motive and conformist impulse. If this were clear, we might then be free to say that one of Hardy's greatest achievements was his skill in overcoming them, even escaping them, and in seeming generally elusive.

Hardy himself wanted us to think of him as a slippery customer. In his first collection, *Wessex Poems* (1898), the contents are clearly divided into different sorts of work – personal/anecdotal, narrative, local, war – which helps to disguise intimate references to the self. In his next two books, the same thing happens more obviously, first in the Preface to *Poems of the Past and the Present* (1901) where he says: 'Of the subject-matter of this volume – even that which is in other than narrative form – much is dramatic or impersonative even where not explicitly so', and then in the Preface to *Time's Laughingstocks* (1909) where he tells us the poems 'are to be regarded, in the main, as dramatic monologues by different characters'.

Hardy had personal reasons for making this emphasis. It also served a large poetic purpose. No English poet since John Clare had a sharper eye for his surroundings ('Afterwards' says it all), but he knew that the effect of his watchfulness depended on his leaving readers well alone. He dissolves his personality into the scene he describes. The process involves a re-creation of self, not an annihilation of self. 'The poetry of a scene varies with the minds of the perceivers', he insisted, 'indeed, it does not lie in the scene at all.' We know what he means as soon as we think of the opening lines in one of his best early poems, 'Neutral Tones':

> We stood by a pond that winter day,
> And the sun was white, as though chidden of God,

And a few leaves lay on the starving sod;
  – They had fallen from an ash, and were gray.

It is a common practice for Romantic artists to interpret
everything in the world around them as a gigantic pathetic
fallacy. In Hardy's case, though, the process is diversified by
psychological forces which turn sympathy with the external
world into an obsession with silence, disappearance, absence,
dissolution. We can see them at work, for instance, in his
fascination with non-communication in the innumerable tragic
narratives and lyrics dealing with love thwarted or misled; or in
his addiction to secrecy, which emerges sometimes as a form of
social self-protection, sometimes as a necessary artistic dissocia-
tion; or in the large number of poems mentioning ghosts, and
others in which he seems to be ghosting and floating himself –
'a spectre not solid enough to influence my environment'; or in
the love poems which suggest something in his personality that
is easily embarrassed and therefore eagerly voyeuristic, sometimes to the extent of seeming actually exploitative, as in 'The
Photograph':

The flame crept up the portrait line by line
As it lay on the coals in the silence of night's profound,
  And over the arm's incline,
And along the marge of the silkwork superfine,
And gnawed at the delicate bosom's defenceless round.

There is another, even more important kind of elusiveness,
important in the sense that it affects a larger number of poems,
and takes us still deeper into the workings of Hardy's imagination. It concerns the evanescence of the present moment, and
especially of happiness in the present moment (his admired
Browning called it 'the good minute'). Although Hardy watches
the present like a hawk (Auden's phrase), he is always quiver-
ingly vulnerable to the past. He is harried by the separation of
now and *then*, particularly when speaking about love, but also
tormented by the way in which different time zones collide with
each other, creating a spark-shower of ironies and disparities.
Hardy enlists the whole of his visible world, and all his invented
worlds as well, to dramatize this division and this joining; each
of his roads, trees, rocks, stiles, fields, hills, woods and houses
reminds him that nothing can be said definitely, nothing felt for
the last time. We can prove the point by opening his poems

almost wherever we like. At 'Under High-Stoy Hill', for instance:

> The moon still meets that tree-tipped height,
> The road – as then – still trails inclined;
>   But since that night
> We have well learnt what lay behind!
>
> For all of the four then climbing here
> But one are ghosts, and he brow-lined;
>   With him they fare,
> Yet speak not of what lies behind.

To say that Hardy is suspended between past and present in many poems, recognizing both time schemes but belonging entirely to neither, might sound like a definition of his melancholy. Yet when his feelings are most poignantly divided and his interests most balanced, his poems are most intense. At moments when other writers might feel compromised he is secure; when others might be overwhelmed his imagination discovers its greatest freedom.

We can see this happening in all categories of poem – in war poems like 'Drummer Hodge' or the brilliant lyric from *The Dynasts* which begins 'The eyelids of eve fall together at last'; in narrative poems like 'A Trampwoman's Tragedy'; in elegies like 'Thoughts of Phena'; in introspective lyrics like 'The Self-Unseeing' or 'I Look Into My Glass'; in poems which were initially occasional like 'The Darkling Thrush' or 'The Convergence of the Twain'. All these bring Hardy into his own by reminding him that he is secure nowhere. He makes each scene intimate, even the most public, but stands outside it. He understands the lessons of history but knows they are generally ignored. He is comforted by a sense of continuity, but simultaneously wounded by feelings of division.

These paradoxes are most obvious, and most creative, in the poems he wrote after the death of his first wife Emma in 1912. He collected most of them in the series 'Poems of 1912–13' which he included in the volume *Satires of Circumstance* (1914), but there are others, too, scattered through subsequent books. Once he had lost Emma he never neglected her, even to the extent of exasperating and depressing his second wife, Florence. During Emma's life, however, it had been a different story.

They first met in 1870 when Hardy, then a trainee architect, went to St Juliot in Cornwall to help restore the local church. Emma Gifford was the rector's sister-in-law, and Hardy married her in 1874. To start with, they were happy – they had a 'two-years' idyll' – but soon sank into indifference and bitterness. 'Love lives on propinquity but dies of contact', Hardy wrote in 1889, and over the next twenty-odd years he often treated his wife slightingly, neglectfully. Emma responded by filling her diary with 'bitter denunciations' of Hardy, 'full of venom, hatred and abuse'. According to one witness she arranged them under the heading 'What I think of my husband'. In the few homes they shared during the first part of their life together, and after 1885 in the gloomy fortress of Max Gate, they chipped away at each other. It was not a battle involving large betrayals or physical abuses, but a guerilla war of grim acerbities and avoidances.

Hardy claimed that Emma's death was 'absolutely unexpected'. In fact he had simply overlooked the signs of her final illness, just as he had formerly underestimated her unhappiness. All the same, some element of shock did form part of his complex reaction to her death, a shock which also led him to destroy most of the documentary evidence of her misery. He burned diaries, retold stories and took out his guilty feelings on Florence, who was living in Max Gate within four weeks of Emma's death. The poems he wrote about Emma during this and subsequent months form part of the same process. They were spun out of self-blame, regret and surprised affection. As Hardy struggled to understand these things, his desire to suppress them competing with an equally powerful longing to publicize them, he relied on all the narrative and lyrical techniques he had already tried and tested.

'Poems of 1912–13', therefore, are not a re-invention of self but a full possession of self. Specifically, they use weather, objects in nature and landscape – particularly Emma's 'own' Cornish landscape – to point up the difference between past pleasure and present pain. They exploit his long-standing fascination with ghosts and hauntings. They keep faith with the visible world of actual things, while transforming them into a mythical landscape, a place where 'Nature is played out as a beauty', and place-names, picnic cups, hills, rain-drops, do not merely support an act of memory but carry the impress of the past. As he says in 'At Castle Boterel':

> Primaeval rocks form the road's steep border,
> And much have they faced there, first and last,
> Of the transitory in Earth's long order;
> But what they record in colour and cast
> Is – that we two passed.

Hardy, recalling Shelley, referred to love as 'Heaven's central star', yet he could not see it clearly, or feel its warmth, or follow where it might lead him when it blazed directly into his life. His strongest affections were only aroused when people were dead, things were distant, and desires could not be fulfilled. Inevitably, this leads to the conclusion that Hardy's best poems are in their various ways all elegies, and that the best of these best are the poems to Emma.

Arguing this means contradicting John Bayley's feeling that such a view 'does not really meet the case'. His objection, though, is not to the quality of Hardy's elegies but to their being interpreted as narrowly 'autobiographical'. As we have seen, Hardy went to great lengths to disguise the story of his life in general and his marriage in particular, but thanks to biographers like Robert Gittings and Michael Millgate we now know a good deal about him. It would be easy, therefore, to read his poems – especially his 'Poems 1912–13' – as if they were merely helpless emissions of personality.

If we did this, we would be assuming there is no difference between the circumstances of a life and the work which arises from it. We would be ignoring what Hardy himself called 'the art of concealing art'. At the same time we can controversially accept that there are sometimes connections between circumstances and work, in Hardy as in every writer, and admit that biography can function as a useful form of criticism. But it must always behave humbly. It must always be alert to separations between life and art, to the way art seeks to make the particular general.

Time and again, Hardy manages this transmutation. We value his best poems so highly because they are written with thrilling intimacy while telling us large truths about our lives – about hope, time and love. In some respects, their geography may now seem remote to us, but the emotions it embodies are ones we still recognize. To some eyes, their metrical forms may seem dated, but when we look at them closely we can see they are always enlivened and made modern by irregularities. We can accept that in certain poems his pessimism is too fixed to be interesting, and in others his manner too mannered, but we can also agree that his best work fills a fat book. Reading it, we begin by thinking that all we can hear is the sort of low-key voice we normally associate with minor poetry – or at least not-major poetry; long before the end, we realize that this same voice is also capable of greatness.

ANDREW MOTION

NOTE ON THE TEXT

The texts of the poems in this Everyman edition are taken from *Thomas Hardy: The Complete Poems*, edited by James Gibson, originally published by Macmillan in 1976, then reissued with corrections in 1978.

Hardy first published a *Collected Poems* in 1919, by which time he had brought out five individual volumes: *Wessex Poems* (1898), *Poems of the Past and the Present* (1901), *Time's Laughingstocks* (1909), *Satires of Circumstance* (1914) and *Moments of Vision* (1917). A second edition of the *Collected Poems* appeared in 1923, adding *Late Lyrics and Earlier* (1922); a third edition, which included *Human Shows* (1925) was published in 1928. Finally, a fourth edition of the *Collected Poems* came out in 1930 and included the posthumous *Winter Words* (1928).

This 1930 edition of the *Collected Poems* reprinted steadily, until James Gibson published *The Complete Poems* in 1976. This edition added 'all the previously uncollected poems' and 'six extracts from *The Dynasts* to which Hardy himself gave the status of separate poems by including them in his *Selected Poems* (1916)'. It also took 'the opportunity' of 'checking the 1930 text, incorporating 'a small number of errors overlooked by Hardy' in the volumes published during his lifetime, 'and by those who checked the [posthumous] 1930 edition'. Furthermore, Gibson incorporated revisions that Hardy had made to his poems once they had appeared in the various editions of the *Collected Poems*. He found, he said, 'plentiful evidence . . . to support Florence Hardy's comment that her husband was artistically unable "to rest content with anything he wrote until he had brought the expression as near to his thought as language would allow"'.

In 1979 Gibson also published a *Variorum Complete Poems of Thomas Hardy*, giving all printed and all significant MS variants. These also appear in Samuel Hynes's edition of *The Complete Poetical Works of Thomas Hardy* (Oxford, 1982 *et seq.*), which includes *The Dynasts* as volumes 4 and 5.

from
WESSEX POEMS
AND OTHER VERSES

Hap

If but some vengeful god would call to me
From up the sky, and laugh: 'Thou suffering thing,
Know that thy sorrow is my ecstasy,
That thy love's loss is my hate's profiting!'

Then would I bear it, clench myself, and die,
Steeled by the sense of ire unmerited;
Half-eased in that a Powerfuller than I
Had willed and meted me the tears I shed.

But not so. How arrives it joy lies slain,
And why unblooms the best hope ever sown?
– Crass Casualty obstructs the sun and rain,
And dicing Time for gladness casts a moan. . . .
These purblind Doomsters had as readily strown
Blisses about my pilgrimage as pain.

1866

Postponement

Snow-bound in woodland, a mournful word,
Dropt now and then from the bill of a bird,
Reached me on wind-wafts; and thus I heard,
        Wearily waiting: –

'I planned her a nest in a leafless tree,
But the passers eyed and twitted me,
And said: "How reckless a bird is he,
        Cheerily mating!"

'Fear-filled, I stayed me till summer-tide,
In lewth of leaves to throne her bride;
But alas! her love for me waned and died,
        Wearily waiting.

'Ah, had I been like some I see,
Born to an evergreen nesting-tree,*
None had eyed and twitted me,
            Cheerily mating!'

1866

Neutral Tones*

We stood by a pond that winter day,
And the sun was white, as though chidden of God,
And a few leaves lay on the starving sod;
      – They had fallen from an ash, and were gray.

Your eyes on me were as eyes that rove
Over tedious riddles of years ago;
And some words played between us to and fro
      On which lost the more by our love.

The smile on your mouth was the deadest thing
Alive enough to have strength to die;
And a grin of bitterness swept thereby
      Like an ominous bird a-wing. . . .

Since then, keen lessons that love deceives,
And wrings with wrong, have shaped to me
Your face, and the God-curst sun, and a tree,
      And a pond edged with grayish leaves.

1867

She at His Funeral

They bear him to his resting-place –
In slow procession sweeping by;
I follow at a stranger's space;
His kindred they, his sweetheart I.

Unchanged my gown of garish dye,
Though sable-sad is their attire;
But they stand round with griefless eye,
Whilst my regret consumes like fire!

187-*

She, to Him 1*

When you shall see me in the toils of Time,
My lauded beauties carried off from me,
My eyes no longer stars as in their prime,
My name forgot of Maiden Fair and Free;

When, in your being, heart concedes to mind,
And judgment, though you scarce its process know,
Recalls the excellencies I once enshrined,
And you are irked that they have withered so:

Remembering mine the loss is, not the blame,
That Sportsman Time but rears his brood to kill,
Knowing me in my soul the very same –
One who would die to spare you touch of ill! –
Will you not grant to old affection's claim
The hand of friendship down Life's sunless hill?

1866

Valenciennes

(1793)

By Corp'l Tullidge, in 'The Trumpet-Major'

IN MEMORY OF S.C. (PENSIONER). DIED 184–

We trenched, we trumpeted and drummed,
And from our mortars tons of iron hummed
Ath'art the ditch, the month we bombed
The Town o' Valencieën.

'Twas in the June o' Ninety-dree
(The Duke o' Yark our then Commander beën)
The German Legion, Guards, and we
        Laid siege to Valencieën.

This was the first time in the war
That French and English spilled each other's gore;
    — Few dreamt how far would roll the roar
        Begun at Valencieën!

'Twas said that we'd no business there
A-topperèn the French for disagreën;
    However, that's not my affair —
        We were at Valencieën.

Such snocks and slats, since war began
Never knew raw recruit or veteràn:
    Stone-deaf therence went many a man
        Who served at Valencieën.

Into the streets, ath'art the sky,
A hundred thousand balls and bombs were fleën;
    And harmless townsfolk fell to die
        Each hour at Valencieën!

And, sweatèn wi' the bombardiers,
A shell was slent to shards anighst my ears:
    — 'Twas nigh the end of hopes and fears
        For me at Valencieën!

They bore my wownded frame to camp,
And shut my gapèn skull, and washed en cleän,
    And jined en wi' a zilver clamp
        Thik night at Valencieën.

'We've fetched en back to quick from dead;
But never more on earth while rose is red
    Will drum rouse Corpel!' Doctor said
        O' me at Valencieën.

'Twer true. No voice o' friend or foe
Can reach me now, or any livèn beën;
    And little have I power to know
      Since then at Valencieën!

I never hear the zummer hums
O' bees; and don' know when the cuckoo comes;
    But night and day I hear the bombs
      We threw at Valencieën. . . .

As for the Duke o' Yark in war,
There may be volk whose judgment o' en is meän;
    But this I say – he was not far
      From great at Valencieën.

O' wild wet nights, when all seems sad,
My wownds come back, as though new wownds I'd had;
    But yet – at times I'm sort o' glad
      I fout at Valencieën.

Well: Heaven wi' its jasper halls
Is now the on'y Town I care to be in. . . .
    Good Lord, if Nick should bomb the walls
      As we did Valencieën!

1878–1897

Her Death and After*

The summons was urgent: and forth I went –
By the way of the Western Wall, so drear
On that winter night, and sought a gate,
    Where one, by Fate,
    Lay dying that I held dear.

And there, as I paused by her tenement,
And the trees shed on me their rime and hoar,
I thought of the man who had left her lone –
    Him who made her his own
    When I loved her, long before.

The rooms within had the piteous shine
That home-things wear when there's aught amiss;
From the stairway floated the rise and fall
   Of an infant's call,
  Whose birth had brought her to this.

Her life was the price she would pay for that whine –
For a child by the man she did not love.
'But let that rest for ever,' I said,
   And bent my tread
  To the bedchamber above.

She took my hand in her thin white own,
And smiled her thanks – though nigh too weak –
And made them a sign to leave us there,
   Then faltered, ere
  She could bring herself to speak.

'Just to see you – before I go – he'll condone
Such a natural thing now my time's not much –
When Death is so near it hustles hence
   All passioned sense
  Between woman and man as such!

'My husband is absent. As heretofore
The City detains him. But, in truth,
He has not been kind. . . . I will speak no blame,
   But – the child is lame;
  O, I pray she may reach his ruth!

'Forgive past days – I can say no more –
Maybe had we wed you would now repine! . . .
But I treated you ill. I was punished. Farewell!
   – Truth shall I tell?
  Would the child were yours and mine!

'As a wife I was true. But, such my unease
That, could I insert a deed back in Time,
I'd make her yours, to secure your care;
   And the scandal bear,
  And the penalty for the crime!'

– When I had left, and the swinging trees
Rang above me, as lauding her candid say,
Another was I. Her words were enough:
        Came smooth, came rough,
    I felt I could live my day.

Next night she died; and her obsequies
In the Field of Tombs where the earthworks frowned
Had her husband's heed. His tendance spent,
        I often went
    And pondered by her mound.

All that year and the next year whiled,
And I still went thitherward in the gloam;
But the Town forgot her and her nook,
        And her husband took
    Another Love to his home.

And the rumour flew that the lame lone child
Whom she wished for its safety child of mine,
Was treated ill when offspring came
        Of the new-made dame,
    And marked a more vigorous line.

A smarter grief within me wrought
Than even at loss of her so dear –
That the being whose soul my soul suffused
        Had a child ill-used,
    While I dared not interfere!

One eve as I stood at my spot of thought
In the white-stoned Garth, brooding thus her wrong,
Her husband neared; and to shun his nod
        By her hallowed sod
    I went from the tombs among

To the Cirque of the Gladiators which faced –
That haggard mark of Imperial Rome,
Whose Pagan echoes mock the chime
        Of our Christian time
    From its hollows of chalk and loam.

The sun's gold touch was scarce displaced
From the vast Arena where men once bled,
When her husband followed; bowed; half-passed
          With lip upcast;
     Then halting sullenly said:

'It is noised that you visit my first wife's tomb.
Now, I gave her an honoured name to bear
While living, when dead. So I've claim to ask
          By what right you task
     My patience by vigiling there?

'There's decency even in death, I assume;
Preserve it, sir, and keep away;
For the mother of my first-born you
          Show mind undue!
     – Sir, I've nothing more to say.'

A desperate stroke discerned I then –
God pardon – or pardon not – the lie;
She had sighed that she wished (lest the child should pine
          Of slights) 'twere mine,
     So I said: 'But the father I.

'That you thought it yours is the way of men;
But I won her troth long ere your day:
You learnt how, in dying, she summoned me?
          'Twas in fealty.
     – Sir, I've nothing more to say,

'Save that, if you'll hand me my little maid,
I'll take her, and rear her, and spare you toil.
Think it more than a friendly act none can;
          I'm a lonely man,
     While you've a large pot to boil.

'If not, and you'll put it to ball or blade –
To-night, to-morrow night, anywhen –
I'll meet you here. . . . But think of it,
          And in season fit
     Let me hear from you again.'

– Well, I went away, hoping; but nought I heard
Of my stroke for the child, till there greeted me
A little voice that one day came
  To my window-frame
  And babbled innocently:

'My father who's not my own, sends word
I'm to stay here, sir, where I belong!'
Next a writing came: 'Since the child was the fruit
  Of your lawless suit,
  Pray take her, to right a wrong.'

And I did. And I gave the child my love,
And the child loved me, and estranged us none.
But compunctions loomed; for I'd harmed the dead
  By what I said
  For the good of the living one.

– Yet though, God wot, I am sinner enough,
And unworthy the woman who drew me so,
Perhaps this wrong for her darling's good
  She forgives, or would,
  If only she could know!

Her Immortality

  Upon a noon I pilgrimed through
   A pasture, mile by mile,
  Unto the place where last I saw
   My dead Love's living smile.

  And sorrowing I lay me down
   Upon the heated sod:
  It seemed as if my body pressed
   The very ground she trod.

  I lay, and thought; and in a trance
   She came and stood thereby –
  The same, even to the marvellous ray
   That used to light her eye.

'You draw me, and I come to you,
   My faithful one,' she said,
In voice that had the moving tone
   It bore ere she was wed.

'Seven years have circled since I died:
   Few now remember me;
My husband clasps another bride:
   My children's love has she.

'My brethren, sisters, and my friends
   Care not to meet my sprite:
Who prized me most I did not know
   Till I passed down from sight.'

I said: 'My days are lonely here;
   I need thy smile alway:
I'll use this night my ball or blade,
   And join thee ere the day.'

A tremor stirred her tender lips,
   Which parted to dissuade:
'That cannot be, O friend,' she cried;
   'Think, I am but a Shade!

'A Shade but in its mindful ones
   Has immortality;
By living, me you keep alive,
   By dying you slay me.

'In you resides my single power
   Of sweet continuance here;
On your fidelity I count
   Through many a coming year.'

– I started through me at her plight,
   So suddenly confessed:
Dismissing late distaste for life,
   I craved its bleak unrest.

'I will not die, my One of all! –
　　To lengthen out thy days
I'll guard me from minutest harms
　　That may invest my ways!'

She smiled and went. Since then she comes
　　Oft when her birth-moon climbs,
Or at the seasons' ingresses,
　　Or anniversary times;

But grows my grief. When I surcease,
　　Through whom alone lives she,
Her spirit ends its living lease,
　　Never again to be!

The Ivy-Wife*

I longed to love a full-boughed beech
　　And be as high as he:
I stretched an arm within his reach,
　　And signalled unity.
But with his drip he forced a breach,
　　And tried to poison me.

I gave the grasp of partnership
　　To one of other race –
A plane: he barked him strip by strip
　　From upper bough to base;
And me therewith; for gone my grip,
　　My arms could not enlace.

In new affection next I strove
　　To coll an ash I saw,
And he in trust received my love;
　　Till with my soft green claw
I cramped and bound him as I wove . . .
　　Such was my love: ha-ha!

By this I gained his strength and height
　　Without his rivalry.

But in my triumph I lost sight
    Of afterhaps. Soon he,
Being bark-bound, flagged, snapped, fell outright,
    And in his fall felled me!

Friends Beyond

William Dewy, Tranter Reuben, Farmer Ledlow late at plough,
    Robert's kin, and John's, and Ned's,
And the Squire, and Lady Susan, lie in Mellstock churchyard now!

'Gone,' I call them, gone for good, that group of local hearts and
    heads;
    Yet at mothy curfew-tide,
And at midnight when the noon-heat breathes it back from walls
    and leads,

They've a way of whispering to me – fellow-wight who yet abide –
    In the muted, measured note
Of a ripple under archways, or a lone cave's stillicide:

'We have triumphed: this achievement turns the bane to antidote,
    Unsuccesses to success,
Many thought-worn eves and morrows to a morrow free of
    thought.

'No more need we corn and clothing, feel of old terrestrial stress;
    Chill detraction stirs no sigh;
Fear of death has even bygone us: death gave all that we possess.'

W.D. – 'Ye mid burn the old bass-viol that I set such value by.'
Squire. – 'You may hold the manse in fee,
    You may wed my spouse, may let my children's memory of
    me die.'

Lady S. – 'You may have my rich brocades, my laces; take each
    household key;
    Ransack coffer, desk, bureau;
    Quiz the few poor treasures hid there, con the letters kept by
    me.'

Far. – 'Ye mid zell my favourite heifer, ye mid let the charlock
    grow,
    Foul the grinterns, give up thrift.'
Far. Wife. – 'If ye break my best blue china, children, I shan't care
    or ho.'

All. – 'We've no wish to hear the tidings, how the people's fortunes
    shift;
    What your daily doings are;
  Who are wedded, born, divided; if your lives beat slow or
    swift.

'Curious not the least are we if our intents you make or mar,
    If you quire to our old tune,
If the City stage still passes, if the weirs still roar afar.'

– Thus, with very gods' composure, freed those crosses late and
    soon
    Which, in life, the Trine allow
(Why, none witteth), and ignoring all that haps beneath the moon,

William Dewy, Tranter Reuben, Farmer Ledlow late at plough,
    Robert's kin, and John's, and Ned's,
And the Squire, and Lady Susan, murmur mildly to me now.

*Thoughts of Phena**
At News of Her Death

  Not a line of her writing have I,
    Not a thread of her hair,
No mark of her late time as dame in her dwelling, whereby
    I may picture her there;
  And in vain do I urge my unsight
    To conceive my lost prize
At her close, whom I knew when her dreams were upbrimming
    with light,
    And with laughter her eyes.

  What scenes spread around her last days,
    Sad, shining, or dim?

Did her gifts and compassions enray and enarch her sweet ways
          With an aureate nimb?*
     Or did life-light decline from her years,
          And mischances control
Her full day-star; unease, or regret, or forebodings, or fears
          Disennoble her soul?

     Thus I do but the phantom retain
          Of the maiden of yore
As my relic; yet haply the best of her – fined in my brain
          It may be the more
     That no line of her writing have I,
          Nor a thread of her hair,
No mark of her late time as dame in her dwelling, whereby
          I may picture her there.

March 1890

Nature's Questioning*

     When I look forth at dawning, pool,
          Field, flock, and lonely tree,
          All seem to gaze at me
Like chastened children sitting silent in a school;

     Their faces dulled, constrained, and worn,
          As though the master's ways
          Through the long teaching days
Had cowed them till their early zest was overborne.

     Upon them stirs in lippings mere
          (As if once clear in call,
          But now scarce breathed at all) –
'We wonder, ever wonder, why we find us here!

     'Has some Vast Imbecility,
          Mighty to build and blend,
          But impotent to tend,
Framed us in jest, and left us now to hazardry?

'Or come we of an Automaton
        Unconscious of our pains? . . .
        Or are we live remains
Of Godhead dying downwards, brain and eye now gone?

'Or is it that some high Plan betides,
        As yet not understood,
        Of Evil stormed by Good,
We the Forlorn Hope over which Achievement strides?'

Thus things around. No answerer I. . . .
        Meanwhile the winds, and rains,
        And Earth's old glooms and pains
Are still the same, and Life and Death are neighbours nigh.

In a Eweleaze near Weatherbury*

The years have gathered grayly
        Since I danced upon this leaze
With one who kindled gaily
        Love's fitful ecstasies!
But despite the term as teacher,
        I remain what I was then
In each essential feature
        Of the fantasies of men.

Yet I note the little chisel
        Of never-napping Time
Defacing wan and grizzel
        The blazon of my prime.
When at night he thinks me sleeping
        I feel him boring sly
Within my bones, and heaping
        Quaintest pains for by-and-by.

Still, I'd go the world with Beauty,
        I would laugh with her and sing,
I would shun divinest duty
        To resume her worshipping.

But she'd scorn my brave endeavour,
  She would not balm the breeze
By murmuring 'Thine for ever!'
  As she did upon this leaze.

1890

I Look Into My Glass*

I look into my glass,
And view my wasting skin,
And say, 'Would God it came to pass
My heart had shrunk as thin!'

For then, I, undistrest
By hearts grown cold to me,
Could lonely wait my endless rest
With equanimity.

But Time, to make me grieve,
Part steals, lets part abide;
And shakes this fragile frame at eve
With throbbings of noontide.

from

POEMS OF THE PAST
AND THE PRESENT

from WAR POEMS

*Drummer Hodge**

i

They throw in Drummer Hodge, to rest
    Uncoffined – just as found:
His landmark is a kopje-crest
    That breaks the veldt around;
And foreign constellations west
    Each night above his mound.

ii

Young Hodge the Drummer never knew –
    Fresh from his Wessex home –
The meaning of the broad Karoo,
    The Bush, the dusty loam,
And why uprose to nightly view
    Strange stars amid the gloam.

iii

Yet portion of that unknown plain
    Will Hodge for ever be;
His homely Northern breast and brain
    Grow to some Southern tree,
And strange-eyed constellations reign
    His stars eternally.

*A Wife in London**

(*December 1899*)

i

She sits in the tawny vapour
    That the Thames-side lanes have uprolled,
    Behind whose webby fold on fold
Like a waning taper
    The street-lamp glimmers cold.

A messenger's knock cracks smartly,
　　Flashed news is in her hand
　　Of meaning it dazes to understand
Though shaped so shortly:
　　He – has fallen – in the far South Land. . . .

ii

'Tis the morrow; the fog hangs thicker,
　　The postman nears and goes:
　　A letter is brought whose lines disclose
By the firelight flicker
　　His hand, whom the worm now knows:

Fresh – firm – penned in highest feather –
　　Page-full of his hoped return,
　　And of home-planned jaunts by brake and burn
In the summer weather,
　　And of new love that they would learn.

from POEMS OF PILGRIMAGE*

*Shelley's Skylark**

(*The neighbourhood of Leghorn: March 1887*)

Somewhere afield here something lies
In Earth's oblivious eyeless trust
That moved a poet to prophecies –
A pinch of unseen, unguarded dust:

The dust of the lark that Shelley heard,
And made immortal through times to be; –
Though it only lived like another bird,
And knew not its immortality:

Lived its meek life; then, one day, fell –
A little ball of feather and bone;
And how it perished, when piped farewell,
And where it wastes, are alike unknown.

Maybe it rests in the loam I view,
Maybe it throbs in a myrtle's green,
Maybe it sleeps in the coming hue
Of a grape on the slopes of yon inland scene.

Go find it, faeries, go and find
That tiny pinch of priceless dust,
And bring a casket silver-lined,
And framed of gold that gems encrust;

And we will lay it safe therein,
And consecrate it to endless time;
For it inspired a bard to win
Ecstatic heights in thought and rhyme.

Lausanne
In Gibbon's Old Garden: 11–12 p.m.

27 June 1897

(The 110th anniversary of the completion of the 'Decline and Fall'
at the same hour and place)

A spirit seems to pass,
Formal in pose, but grave withal and grand:
He contemplates a volume in his hand,
And far lamps fleck him through the thin acacias.

Anon the book is closed,
With 'It is finished!' And at the alley's end
He turns, and when on me his glances bend
As from the Past comes speech – small, muted, yet composed.

'How fares the Truth now? – Ill?
– Do pens but slily further her advance?
May one not speed her but in phrase askance?
Do scribes aver the Comic to be Reverend still?

'Still rule those minds on earth
At whom sage Milton's wormwood words were hurled:
*"Truth like a bastard comes into the world
Never without ill-fame to him who gives her birth"*?'

from MISCELLANEOUS POEMS

A Commonplace Day

The day is turning ghost,
And scuttles from the kalendar in fits and furtively,
To join the anonymous host
Of those that throng oblivion; ceding his place, maybe,
To one of like degree.

I part the fire-gnawed logs,
Rake forth the embers, spoil the busy flames, and lay the ends
Upon the shining dogs;
Further and further from the nooks the twilight's stride extends,
And beamless black impends.

Nothing of tiniest worth
Have I wrought, pondered, planned; no one thing asking blame or
praise,
Since the pale corpse-like birth
Of this diurnal unit, bearing blanks in all its rays –
Dullest of dull-hued Days!

Wanly upon the panes
The rain slides, as have slid since morn my colourless thoughts;
and yet
Here, while Day's presence wanes,
And over him the sepulchre-lid is slowly lowered and set,
He wakens my regret.

Regret – though nothing dear
That I wot of, was toward in the wide world at his prime,
    Or bloomed elsewhere than here,
To die with his decease, and leave a memory sweet, sublime,
    Or mark him out in Time. . . .

    – Yet, maybe, in some soul,
In some spot undiscerned on sea or land, some impulse rose,
    Or some intent upstole
Of that enkindling ardency from whose maturer glows
    The world's amendment flows;

    But which, benumbed at birth
By momentary chance or wile, has missed its hope to be
    Embodied on the earth;
And undervoicings of this loss to man's futurity
    May wake regret in me.

At a Lunar Eclipse

Thy shadow, Earth, from Pole to Central Sea,
Now steals along upon the Moon's meek shine
In even monochrome and curving line
Of imperturbable serenity.

How shall I link such sun-cast symmetry
With the torn troubled form I know as thine,
That profile, placid as a brow divine,
With continents of moil and misery?

And can immense Mortality but throw
So small a shade, and Heaven's high human scheme
Be hemmed within the coasts yon arc implies?

Is such the stellar gauge of earthly show,
Nation at war with nation, brains that teem,
Heroes, and women fairer than the skies?

*To an Unborn Pauper Child**

i

Breathe not, hid Heart: cease silently,
And though thy birth-hour beckons thee,
    Sleep the long sleep:
    The Doomsters heap
Travails and teens around us here,
And Time-wraiths turn our songsingings to fear.

ii

Hark, how the peoples surge and sigh,
And laughters fail, and greetings die:
    Hopes dwindle; yea,
    Faiths waste away,
Affections and enthusiasms numb;
Thou canst not mend these things if thou dost come.

iii

Had I the ear of wombèd souls
Ere their terrestrial chart unrolls,
    And thou wert free
    To cease, or be,
Then would I tell thee all I know,
And put it to thee: Wilt thou take Life so?

iv

Vain vow! No hint of mine may hence
To theeward fly: to thy locked sense
    Explain none can
    Life's pending plan:
Thou wilt thy ignorant entry make
Though skies spout fire and blood and nations quake.

v

Fain would I, dear, find some shut plot
Of earth's wide wold for thee, where not
    One tear, one qualm,
    Should break the calm.
But I am weak as thou and bare;
No man can change the common lot to rare.

vi

Must come and bide. And such are we —
Unreasoning, sanguine, visionary —
    That I can hope
    Health, love, friends, scope
In full for thee; can dream thou'lt find
Joys seldom yet attained by humankind!

*To Lizbie Browne**

i

Dear Lizbie Browne,
Where are you now?
In sun, in rain? —
    Or is your brow
    Past joy, past pain,
Dear Lizbie Browne?

ii

Sweet Lizbie Browne,
How you could smile,
How you could sing! —
    How archly wile
    In glance-giving,
Sweet Lizbie Browne!

iii

And, Lizbie Browne,
Who else had hair
Bay-red as yours,
    Or flesh so fair
    Bred out of doors,
Sweet Lizbie Browne?

iv

When, Lizbie Browne,
You had just begun
To be endeared
    By stealth to one,
    You disappeared
My Lizbie Browne!

v

Ay, Lizbie Browne,
So swift your life,
And mine so slow,
You were a wife
Ere I could show
Love, Lizbie Browne.

vi

Still, Lizbie Browne,
You won, they said,
The best of men
When you were wed. . . .
Where went you then,
O Lizbie Browne?

vii

Dear Lizbie Browne,
I should have thought,
'Girls ripen fast,'
And coaxed and caught
You ere you passed,
Dear Lizbie Browne!

viii

But, Lizbie Browne,
I let you slip;
Shaped not a sign;
Touched never your lip
With lip of mine,
Lost Lizbie Browne!

ix

So, Lizbie Browne,
When on a day
Men speak of me
As not, you'll say,
'And who was he?' —
Yes, Lizbie Browne!

The Well-Beloved*

I went by star and planet shine
    Towards the dear one's home
At Kingsbere, there to make her mine
    When the next sun upclomb.

I edged the ancient hill and wood
    Beside the Ikling Way,
Nigh where the Pagan temple stood
    In the world's earlier day.

And as I quick and quicker walked
    On gravel and on green,
I sang to sky, and tree, or talked
    Of her I called my queen.

– 'O faultless is her dainty form,
    And luminous her mind;
She is the God-created norm
    Of perfect womankind!'

A shape whereon one star-blink gleamed
    Slid softly by my side,
A woman's; and her motion seemed
    The motion of my bride.

And yet methought she'd drawn erstwhile
    Out from the ancient leaze,
Where once were pile and peristyle
    For men's idolatries.

– 'O maiden lithe and lone, what may
    Thy name and lineage be
Who so resemblest by this ray
    My darling? – Art thou she?'

The Shape: 'Thy bride remains within
    Her father's grange and grove.'
– 'Thou speakest rightly,' I broke in,
    'Thou art not she I love.'

– 'Nay: though thy bride remains inside
    Her father's walls,' said she,
'The one most dear is with thee here,
    For thou dost love but me.'

Then I: 'But she, my only choice,
    Is now at Kingsbere Grove?'
Again her soft mysterious voice:
    'I am thy only Love.'

Thus still she vouched, and still I said,
    'O sprite, that cannot be!' . . .
It was as if my bosom bled,
    So much she troubled me.

The sprite resumed: 'Thou hast transferred
    To her dull form awhile
My beauty, fame, and deed, and word,
    My gestures and my smile.

'O fatuous man, this truth infer,
    Brides are not what they seem;
Thou lovest what thou dreamest her;
    I am thy very dream!'

– 'O then,' I answered miserably,
    Speaking as scarce I knew,
'My loved one, I must wed with thee
    If what thou sayest be true!'

She, proudly, thinning in the gloom:
    'Though, since troth-plight began,
I have ever stood as bride to groom,
    I wed no mortal man!'

Thereat she vanished by the lane
    Adjoining Kingsbere town,
Near where, men say, once stood the Fane
    To Venus, on the Down.

– When I arrived and met my bride
    Her look was pinched and thin,
As if her soul had shrunk and died,
    And left a waste within.

A Broken Appointment*

You did not come,
And marching Time drew on, and wore me numb. –
Yet less for loss of your dear presence there
Than that I thus found lacking in your make
That high compassion which can overbear
Reluctance for pure lovingkindness' sake
Grieved I, when, as the hope-hour stroked its sum,
    You did not come.

You love not me,
And love alone can lend you loyalty;
– I know and knew it. But, unto the store
Of human deeds divine in all but name,
Was it not worth a little hour or more
To add yet this: Once you, a woman, came
To soothe a time-torn man; even though it be
    You love not me?

Between Us Now

Between us now and here –
    Two thrown together
Who are not wont to wear
    Life's flushest feather –
Who see the scenes slide past,
The daytimes dimming fast,
Let there be truth at last,
    Even if despair.

So thoroughly and long
    Have you now known me,

So real in faith and strong
        Have I now shown me,
That nothing needs disguise
Further in any wise,
Or asks or justifies
        A guarded tongue.

Face unto face, then, say,
        Eyes my own meeting,
Is your heart far away,
        Or with mine beating?
When false things are brought low,
And swift things have grown slow,
Feigning like froth shall go,
        Faith be for aye.

I Need Not Go

I need not go
Through sleet and snow
To where I know
She waits for me;
She will tarry me there
Till I find it fair,
And have time to spare
From company.

When I've overgot
The world somewhat,
When things cost not
Such stress and strain,
Is soon enough
By cypress sough
To tell my Love
I am come again.

And if some day,
When none cries nay,
I still delay
To seek her side,

(Though ample measure
Of fitting leisure
Await my pleasure)
She will not chide.

What – not upbraid me
That I delayed me,
Nor ask what stayed me
So long? Ah, no! –
New cares may claim me,
New loves inflame me,
She will not blame me,
But suffer it so.

His Immortality

i

I saw a dead man's finer part
Shining within each faithful heart
Of those bereft. Then said I: 'This must be
    His immortality.'

ii

I looked there as the seasons wore,
And still his soul continuously bore
A life in theirs. But less its shine excelled
    Than when I first beheld.

iii

His fellow-yearsmen passed, and then
In later hearts I looked for him again;
And found him – shrunk, alas! into a thin
    And spectral mannikin.

iv

Lastly I ask – now old and chill –
If aught of him remain unperished still;
And find, in me alone, a feeble spark,
    Dying amid the dark.

February 1899

Wives in the Sere

i

Never a careworn wife but shows,
    If a joy suffuse her,
Something beautiful to those
    Patient to peruse her,
Some one charm the world unknows
    Precious to a muser,
Haply what, ere years were foes,
    Moved her mate to choose her.

ii

But, be it a hint of rose
    That an instant hues her,
Or some early light or pose
    Wherewith thought renews her –
Seen by him at full, ere woes
    Practised to abuse her –
Sparely comes it, swiftly goes,
    Time again subdues her.

An August Midnight

i

A shaded lamp and a waving blind,
And the beat of a clock from a distant floor:
On this scene enter – winged, horned, and spined –
A longlegs, a moth, and a dumbledore;
While 'mid my page there idly stands
A sleepy fly, that rubs its hands . . .

ii

Thus meet we five, in this still place,
At this point of time, at this point in space.
– My guests besmear my new-penned line,
Or bang at the lamp and fall supine.
'God's humblest, they!' I muse. Yet why?
They know Earth-secrets that know not I.

Max Gate, 1899

The Darkling Thrush*

I leant upon a coppice gate
    When Frost was spectre-gray,
And Winter's dregs made desolate
    The weakening eye of day.
The tangled bine-stems scored the sky
    Like strings of broken lyres,
And all mankind that haunted nigh
    Had sought their household fires.

The land's sharp features seemed to be
    The Century's corpse outleant,
His crypt the cloudy canopy,
    The wind his death-lament.
The ancient pulse of germ and birth
    Was shrunken hard and dry,
And every spirit upon earth
    Seemed fervourless as I.

At once a voice arose among
    The bleak twigs overhead
In a full-hearted evensong
    Of joy illimited;
An aged thrush, frail, gaunt, and small,
    In blast-beruffled plume,
Had chosen thus to fling his soul
    Upon the growing gloom.

So little cause for carolings
    Of such ecstatic sound
Was written on terrestrial things
    Afar or nigh around,
That I could think there trembled through
    His happy good-night air
Some blessed Hope, whereof he knew
    And I was unaware.

31 December 1900

A Wasted Illness

Through vaults of pain,
Enribbed and wrought with groins of ghastliness,
I passed, and garish spectres moved my brain
          To dire distress.

And hammerings,
And quakes, and shoots, and stifling hotness, blent
With webby waxing things and waning things
          As on I went.

'Where lies the end
To this foul way?' I asked with weakening breath.
Thereon ahead I saw a door extend –
          The door to Death.

It loomed more clear:
'At last!' I cried. 'The all-delivering door!'
And then, I knew not how, it grew less near
          Than theretofore.

And back slid I
Along the galleries by which I came,
And tediously the day returned, and sky,
          And life – the same.

And all was well:
Old circumstance resumed its former show,
And on my head the dews of comfort fell
          As ere my woe.

I roam anew,
Scarce conscious of my late distress. . . . And yet
Those backward steps to strength I cannot view
          Without regret.

For that dire train
Of waxing shapes and waning, passed before,
And those grim chambers, must be ranged again
          To reach that door.

The Ruined Maid

'O 'Melia, my dear, this does everything crown!
Who could have supposed I should meet you in Town?
And whence such fair garments, such prosperi-ty?' –
'O didn't you know I'd been ruined?' said she.

– 'You left us in tatters, without shoes or socks,
Tired of digging potatoes, and spudding up docks;
And now you've gay bracelets and bright feathers three!' –
'Yes: that's how we dress when we're ruined,' said she.

– 'At home in the barton you said "thee" and "thou",
And "thik oon", and "theäs oon", and "t'other"; but now
Your talking quite fits 'ee for high compa-ny!' –
'Some polish is gained with one's ruin,' said she.

– 'Your hands were like paws then, your face blue and bleak
But now I'm bewitched by your delicate cheek,
And your little gloves fit as on any la-dy!' –
'We never do work when we're ruined,' said she.

– 'You used to call home-life a hag-ridden dream,
And you'd sigh, and you'd sock; but at present you seem
To know not of megrims or melancho-ly!' –
'True. One's pretty lively when ruined,' said she.

– 'I wish I had feathers, a fine sweeping gown,
And a delicate face, and could strut about Town!' –
'My dear – a raw country girl, such as you be,
Cannot quite expect that. You ain't ruined,' said she.

Westbourne Park Villas, 1866

The Self-Unseeing*

Here is the ancient floor,
Footworn and hollowed and thin,
Here was the former door
Where the dead feet walked in.

She sat here in her chair,
Smiling into the fire;
He who played stood there,
Bowing it higher and higher.

Childlike, I danced in a dream;
Blessings emblazoned that day;
Everything glowed with a gleam;
Yet we were looking away!

In Tenebris 1*

'Percussus sum sicut fœnum, et aruit cor meum.' – Ps. CI

Wintertime nighs;
But my bereavement-pain
It cannot bring again:
    Twice no one dies.

Flower-petals flee;
But, since it once hath been,
No more that severing scene
    Can harrow me.

Birds faint in dread:
I shall not lose old strength
In the lone frost's black length:
    Strength long since fled!

Leaves freeze to dun;
But friends can not turn cold
This season as of old
    For him with none.

Tempests may scath;
But love can not make smart
Again this year his heart
    Who no heart hath.

Black is night's cope;
But death will not appal
One who, past doubtings all,
Waits in unhope.

from

TIME'S LAUGHINGSTOCKS
AND OTHER VERSES

A Trampwoman's Tragedy*

(182–)

i

From Wynyard's Gap the livelong day,
 The livelong day,
We beat afoot the northward way
 We had travelled times before.
The sun-blaze burning on our backs,
Our shoulders sticking to our packs,
By fosseway, fields, and turnpike tracks
 We skirted sad Sedge-Moor.

ii

Full twenty miles we jaunted on,
 We jaunted on, –
My fancy-man, and jeering John,
 And Mother Lee, and I.
And, as the sun drew down to west,
We climbed the toilsome Poldon crest,
And saw, of landskip sights the best,
 The inn that beamed thereby.

iii

For months we had padded side by side,
 Ay, side by side
Through the Great Forest, Blackmoor wide,
 And where the Parret ran.
We'd faced the gusts on Mendip ridge,
Had crossed the Yeo unhelped by bridge,
Been stung by every Marshwood midge,
 I and my fancy-man.

iv

Lone inns we loved, my man and I,
 My man and I;
'King's Stag', 'Windwhistle' high and dry,
 'The Horse' on Hintock Green,
The cosy house at Wynyard's Gap,
'The Hut' renowned on Bredy Knap,

And many another wayside tap
　　Where folk might sit unseen.

v

Now as we trudged – O deadly day,
　　O deadly day! –
I teased my fancy-man in play
　　And wanton idleness.
I walked alongside jeering John,
I laid his hand my waist upon;
I would not bend my glances on
　　My lover's dark distress.

vi

Thus Poldon top at last we won,
　　At last we won,
And gained the inn at sink of sun
　　Far-famed as 'Marshal's Elm'.
Beneath us figured tor and lea,
From Mendip to the western sea –
I doubt if finer sight there be
　　Within this royal realm.

vii

Inside the settle all a-row –
　　All four a-row
We sat, I next to John, to show
　　That he had wooed and won.
And then he took me on his knee,
And swore it was his turn to be
My favoured mate, and Mother Lee
　　Passed to my former one.

viii

Then in a voice I had never heard,
　　I had never heard,
My only Love to me: 'One word,
　　My lady, if you please!
Whose is the child you are like to bear? –
His? After all my months o' care?'

God knows 'twas not! But, O despair!
    I nodded – still to tease.

ix

Then up he sprung, and with his knife –
    And with his knife
He let out jeering Johnny's life,
    Yes; there, at set of sun.
The slant ray through the window nigh
Gilded John's blood and glazing eye,
Ere scarcely Mother Lee and I
    Knew that the deed was done.

x

The taverns tell the gloomy tale,
    The gloomy tale,
How that at Ivel-chester jail
    My Love, my sweetheart swung;
Though stained till now by no misdeed
Save one horse ta'en in time o' need;
(Blue Jimmy stole right many a steed
    Ere his last fling he flung.)

xi

Thereaft I walked the world alone,
    Alone, alone!
On his death-day I gave my groan
    And dropt his dead-born child.
'Twas nigh the jail, beneath a tree,
None tending me; for Mother Lee
Had died at Glaston, leaving me
    Unfriended on the wild.

xii

And in the night as I lay weak,
    As I lay weak,
The leaves a-falling on my cheek,
    The red moon low declined –
The ghost of him I'd die to kiss
Rose up and said: 'Ah, tell me this!

Was the child mine, or was it his?
      Speak, that I rest may find!'

              xiii
O doubt not but I told him then,
      I told him then,
That I had kept me from all men
      Since we joined lips and swore.
Whereat he smiled, and thinned away
As the wind stirred to call up day . . .
— 'Tis past! And here alone I stray
      Haunting the Western Moor.

NOTES – 'Windwhistle' (Stanza iv). The highness and dryness of Windwhistle Inn was
impressed upon the writer two or three years ago, when, after climbing on a hot afternoon
to the beautiful spot near which it stands and entering the inn for tea, he was informed by
the landlady that none could be had, unless he would fetch water from a valley half a mile
off, the house containing not a drop, owing to its situation. However, a tantalizing row of
full barrels behind her back testified to a wetness of a certain sort, which was not at that
time desired.

'Marshal's Elm' (Stanza vi), so picturesquely situated, is no longer an inn, though the
house, or part of it, still remains. It used to exhibit a fine old swinging sign.

'Blue Jimmy' (Stanza x) was a notorious horse-stealer of Wessex in those days, who
appropriated more than a hundred horses before he was caught, among others one
belonging to a neighbour of the writer's grandfather. He was hanged at the now demolished
Ivelchester or Ilchester jail above mentioned – that building formerly of so many sinister
associations in the minds of the local peasantry, and the continual haunt of fever, which at
last led to its condemnation.

Its site is now an innocent-looking green meadow.

April 1902

A Sunday Morning Tragedy*

(*circa 186–*)

I bore a daughter flower-fair,
In Pydel Vale, alas for me;
I joyed to mother one so rare,
But dead and gone I now would be.

Men looked and loved her as she grew,
And she was won, alas for me;
She told me nothing, but I knew,
And saw that sorrow was to be.

I knew that one had made her thrall,
A thrall to him, alas for me;
And then, at last, she told me all,
And wondered what her end would be.

She owned that she had loved too well,
Had loved too well, unhappy she,
And bore a secret time would tell,
Though in her shroud she'd sooner be.

I plodded to her sweetheart's door
In Pydel Vale, alas for me:
I pleaded with him, pleaded sore,
To save her from her misery.

He frowned, and swore he could not wed,
Seven times he swore it could not be;
'Poverty's worse than shame,' he said,
Till all my hope went out of me.

'I've packed my traps to sail the main' —
Roughly he spake, alas did he —
'Wessex beholds me not again,
'Tis worse than any jail would be!'

— There was a shepherd whom I knew,
A subtle man, alas for me:
I sought him all the pastures through,
Though better I had ceased to be.

I traced him by his lantern light,
And gave him hint, alas for me,
Of how she found her in the plight
That is so scorned in Christendie.

'Is there an herb . . . ?' I asked. 'Or none?'
Yes, thus I asked him desperately.
' — There is,' he said; 'a certain one. . . .'
Would he had sworn that none knew he!

'To-morrow I will walk your way,'
He hinted low, alas for me. –
Fieldwards I gazed throughout next day;
Now fields I never more would see!

The sunset-shine, as curfew strook,
As curfew strook beyond the lea,
Lit his white smock and gleaming crook,
While slowly he drew near to me.

He pulled from underneath his smock
The herb I sought, my curse to be –
'At times I use it in my flock,'
He said, and hope waxed strong in me.

''Tis meant to balk ill-motherings' –
(Ill-motherings! Why should they be?) –
'If not, would God have sent such things?'
So spoke the shepherd unto me.

That night I watched the poppling brew,
With bended back and hand on knee:
I stirred it till the dawnlight grew,
And the wind whiffled wailfully.

'This scandal shall be slain,' said I,
'That lours upon her innocency:
I'll give all whispering tongues the lie;' –
But worse than whispers was to be.

'Here's physic for untimely fruit,'
I said to her, alas for me,
Early that morn in fond salute;
And in my grave I now would be.

– Next Sunday came, with sweet church chimes
In Pydel Vale, alas for me:
I went into her room betimes;
No more may such a Sunday be!

'Mother, instead of rescue nigh,'
She faintly breathed, alas for me,
'I feel as I were like to die,
And underground soon, soon should be.'

From church that noon the people walked
In twos and threes, alas for me,
Showed their new raiment — smiled and talked,
Though sackcloth-clad I longed to be.

Came to my door her lover's friends,
And cheerly cried, alas for me,
'Right glad are we he makes amends,
For never a sweeter bride can be.'

My mouth dried, as 'twere scorched within,
Dried at their words, alas for me:
More and more neighbours crowded in,
(O why should mothers ever be!)

'Ha-ha! Such well-kept news!' laughed they,
Yes — so they laughed, alas for me.
'Whose banns were called in church to-day?' —
Christ, how I wished my soul could flee!

'Where is she? O the stealthy miss,'
Still bantered they, alas for me,
'To keep a wedding close as this. . . .'
Ay, Fortune worked thus wantonly!

'But you are pale — you did not know?'
They archly asked, alas for me,
I stammered, 'Yes — some days — ago,'
While coffined clay I wished to be.

''Twas done to please her, we surmise?'
(They spoke quite lightly in their glee)
'Done by him as a fond surprise?'
I thought their words would madden me.

Her lover entered. 'Where's my bird? –
My bird – my flower – my picotee?
First time of asking, soon the third!'
Ah, in my grave I well may be.

To me he whispered: 'Since your call – '
So spoke he then, alas for me –
'I've felt for her, and righted all.'
– I think of it to agony.

'She's faint to-day – tired – nothing more – '
Thus did I lie, alas for me. . . .
I called her at her chamber door
As one who scarce had strength to be.

No voice replied. I went within –
O women! scourged the worst are we. . . .
I shrieked. The others hastened in
And saw the stroke there dealt on me.

There she lay – silent, breathless, dead,
Stone dead she lay – wronged, sinless she! –
Ghost-white the cheeks once rosy-red:
Death had took her. Death took not me.

I kissed her colding face and hair,
I kissed her corpse – the bride to be! –
My punishment I cannot bear,
But pray God *not* to pity me.

January 1904

The Curate's Kindness

A Workhouse Irony

i

I thought they'd be strangers aroun' me,
    But she's to be there!
Let me jump out o' waggon and go back and drown me
    At Pummery or Ten-Hatches Weir.

ii

I thought: 'Well, I've come to the Union – *
    The workhouse at last –
After honest hard work all the week, and Communion
    O' Zundays, these fifty years past.

iii

''Tis hard; but,' I thought, 'never mind it:
    There's gain in the end:
And when I get used to the place I shall find it
    A home, and may find there a friend.

iv

'Life there will be better than t'other,
    For peace is assured.
The men in one wing and their wives in another
    Is strictly the rule of the Board.'

v

Just then one young Pa'son arriving
    Steps up out of breath
To the side o' the waggon wherein we were driving
    To Union; and calls out and saith:

vi

'Old folks, that harsh order is altered,
    Be not sick of heart!
The Guardians they poohed and they pished and they paltered
    When urged not to keep you apart.

vii

' "It is wrong," I maintained, "to divide them,
    Near forty years wed."
"Very well, sir. We promise, then, they shall abide them
    In one wing together," they said.'

viii

Then I sank – knew 'twas quite a foredone thing
    That misery should be
To the end!. . . To get freed of her there was the one thing
    Had made the change welcome to me.

ix

To go there was ending but badly;
    'Twas shame and 'twas pain;
'But anyhow,' thought I, 'thereby I shall gladly
    Get free of this forty years' chain.'

x

I thought they'd be strangers aroun' me,
    But she's to be there!
Let me jump out o' waggon and go back and drown me
    At Pummery or Ten-Hatches Weir.

Shut Out That Moon

Close up the casement, draw the blind,
    Shut out that stealing moon,
She wears too much the guise she wore
    Before our lutes were strewn
With years-deep dust, and names we read
    On a white stone were hewn.

Step not forth on the dew-dashed lawn
    To view the Lady's Chair,
Immense Orion's glittering form,
    The Less and Greater Bear:
Stay in; to such sights we were drawn
    When faded ones were fair.

Brush not the bough for midnight scents
    That come forth lingeringly,
And wake the same sweet sentiments
    They breathed to you and me
When living seemed a laugh, and love
    All it was said to be.

Within the common lamp-lit room
    Prison my eyes and thought;
Let dingy details crudely loom,
    Mechanic speech be wrought:

Too fragrant was Life's early bloom,
　　Too tart the fruit it brought!

1904

The Dead Man Walking*

They hail me as one living,
　　But don't they know
That I have died of late years,
　　Untombed although?

I am but a shape that stands here,
　　A pulseless mould,
A pale past picture, screening
　　Ashes gone cold.

Not at a minute's warning,
　　Not in a loud hour,
For me ceased Time's enchantments
　　In hall and bower.

There was no tragic transit,
　　No catch of breath,
When silent seasons inched me
　　On to this death. . . .

– A Troubadour-youth I rambled
　　With Life for lyre,
The beats of being raging
　　In me like fire.

But when I practised eyeing
　　The goal of men,
It iced me, and I perished
　　A little then.

When passed my friend, my kinsfolk,
　　Through the Last Door,
And left me standing bleakly,
　　I died yet more;

And when my Love's heart kindled
   In hate of me,
Wherefore I knew not, died I
   One more degree.

And if when I died fully
   I cannot say,
And changed into the corpse-thing
   I am to-day;

Yet is it that, though whiling
   The time somehow
In walking, talking, smiling,
   I live not now.

from MORE LOVE LYRICS

On the Departure Platform

We kissed at the barrier; and passing through
She left me, and moment by moment got
Smaller and smaller, until to my view
      She was but a spot;

A wee white spot of muslin fluff
That down the diminishing platform bore
Through hustling crowds of gentle and rough
      To the carriage door.

Under the lamplight's fitful glowers,
Behind dark groups from far and near,
Whose interests were apart from ours,
      She would disappear,

Then show again, till I ceased to see
That flexible form, that nebulous white;
And she who was more than my life to me
      Had vanished quite. . . .

We have penned new plans since that fair fond day,
And in season she will appear again —
Perhaps in the same soft white array —
  But never as then!

— 'And why, young man, must eternally fly
A joy you'll repeat, if you love her well?'
— O friend, nought happens twice thus; why,
  I cannot tell!

In a Cathedral City

These people have not heard your name;
No loungers in this placid place
Have helped to bruit your beauty's fame.

The grey Cathedral, towards whose face
Bend eyes untold, has met not yours;
Your shade has never swept its base,

Your form has never darked its doors,
Nor have your faultless feet once thrown
A pensive pit-pat on its floors.

Along the street to maids well known
Blithe lovers hum their tender airs,
But in your praise voice not a tone. . . .

— Since nought bespeaks you here, or bears,
As I, your imprint through and through,
Here might I rest, till my heart shares
The spot's unconsciousness of you!

Salisbury

At Waking

When night was lifting,
And dawn had crept under its shade,
　Amid cold clouds drifting
Dead-white as a corpse outlaid,
　　　With a sudden scare
　　　I seemed to behold
　　　My Love in bare
　　　Hard lines unfold.

　Yea, in a moment,
An insight that would not die
　Killed her old endowment
Of charm that had capped all nigh,
　　　Which vanished to none
　　　Like the gilt of a cloud,
　　　And showed her but one
　　　Of the common crowd.

She seemed but a sample
Of earth's poor average kind,
　Lit up by no ample
Enrichments of mien or mind.
　　　I covered my eyes
　　　As to cover the thought,
　　　And unrecognize
　　　What the morn had taught.

　O vision appalling
When the one believed-in thing
　Is seen falling, falling,
With all to which hope can cling.
　　　Off: it is not true;
　　　For it cannot be
　　　That the prize I drew
　　　Is a blank to me!

Weymouth, 1869

In the Vaulted Way

In the vaulted way, where the passage turned
To the shadowy corner that none could see,
You paused for our parting, – plaintively;
Though overnight had come words that burned
My fond frail happiness out of me.

And then I kissed you, – despite my thought
That our spell must end when reflection came
On what you had deemed me, whose one long aim
Had been to serve you; that what I sought
Lay not in a heart that could breathe such blame.

But yet I kissed you; whereon you again
As of old kissed me. Why, why was it so?
Do you cleave to me after that light-tongued blow?
If you scorned me at eventide, how love then?
The thing is dark, Dear. I do not know.

In the Night She Came

I told her when I left one day
That whatsoever weight of care
Might strain our love, Time's mere assault
      Would work no changes there.
And in the night she came to me,
      Toothless, and wan, and old,
With leaden concaves round her eyes,
      And wrinkles manifold.

I tremblingly exclaimed to her,
'O wherefore do you ghost me thus!
I have said that dull defacing Time
      Will bring no dreads to us.'
'And is that true of *you*?' she cried
      In voice of troubled tune.
I faltered: 'Well . . . I did not think
      You would test me quite so soon!'

She vanished with a curious smile,
Which told me, plainlier than by word,
That my staunch pledge could scarce beguile
    The fear she had averred.
Her doubts then wrought their shape in me,
    And when next day I paid
My due caress, we seemed to be
    Divided by some shade.

He Abjures Love*

At last I put off love,
    For twice ten years
The daysman of my thought,
    And hope, and doing;
Being ashamed thereof,
    And faint of fears
And desolations, wrought
    In his pursuing,

Since first in youthtime those
    Disquietings
That heart-enslavement brings
    To hale and hoary,
Became my housefellows,
    And, fool and blind,
I turned from kith and kind
    To give him glory.

I was as children be
    Who have no care;
I did not shrink or sigh,
    I did not sicken;
But lo, Love beckoned me,
    And I was bare,
And poor, and starved, and dry,
    And fever-stricken.

Too many times ablaze
   With fatuous fires,
Enkindled by his wiles
   To new embraces,
Did I, by wilful ways
   And baseless ires,
Return the anxious smiles
   Of friendly faces.

No more will now rate I
   The common rare,
The midnight drizzle dew,
   The gray hour golden,
The wind a yearning cry,
   The faulty fair,
Things dreamt, of comelier hue
   Than things beholden! . . .

– I speak as one who plumbs
   Life's dim profound,
One who at length can sound
   Clear views and certain.
But – after love what comes?
   A scene that lours,
A few sad vacant hours,
   And then, the Curtain.

1883

from A SET OF COUNTRY SONGS

At Casterbridge Fair
i. The Ballad-Singer

Sing, Ballad-singer, raise a hearty tune;
Make me forget that there was ever a one
I walked with in the meek light of the moon
   When the day's work was done.

Rhyme, Ballad-rhymer, start a country song;
Make me forget that she whom I loved well
Swore she would love me dearly, love me long,
        Then – what I cannot tell!

Sing, Ballad-singer, from your little book;
Make me forget those heart-breaks, achings, fears;
Make me forget her name, her sweet sweet look –
        Make me forget her tears.

vii. After the Fair

The singers are gone from the Cornmarket-place
        With their broadsheets of rhymes,
The street rings no longer in treble and bass
        With their skits on the times,
And the Cross, lately thronged, is a dim naked space
        That but echoes the stammering chimes.

From Clock-corner steps, as each quarter ding-dongs,
        Away the folk roam
By the 'Hart' and Grey's Bridge into byways and 'drongs',
        Or across the ridged loam;
The younger ones shrilling the lately heard songs,
        The old saying, 'Would we were home.'

The shy-seeming maiden so mute in the fair
        Now rattles and talks,
And that one who looked the most swaggering there
        Grows sad as she walks,
And she who seemed eaten by cankering care
        In statuesque sturdiness stalks.

And midnight clears High Street of all but the ghosts
        Of its buried burghees,
From the latest far back to those old Roman hosts
        Whose remains one yet sees,

Who loved, laughed, and fought, hailed their friends, drank
    their toasts
At their meeting-times here, just as these!

1902

NOTE – 'The chimes' (line 6) will be listened for in vain here at midnight now, having been
abolished some years ago.*

from PIECES OCCASIONAL AND
VARIOUS

A Church Romance

(Mellstock: circa 1835)

She turned in the high pew, until her sight
Swept the west gallery, and caught its row
Of music-men with viol, book, and bow
Against the sinking sad tower-window light.

She turned again; and in her pride's despite
One strenuous viol's inspirer seemed to throw
A message from his string to her below,
Which said: 'I claim thee as my own forthright!'

Thus their hearts' bond began, in due time signed.
And long years thence, when Age had scared Romance,
At some old attitude of his or glance
That gallery-scene would break upon her mind,
With him as minstrel, ardent, young, and trim,
Bowing 'New Sabbath' or 'Mount Ephraim'.

A Wife and Another

'War ends, and he's returning
        Early; yea,
The evening next to-morrow's!' –
        – This I say
To her, whom I suspiciously survey,

Holding my husband's letter
        To her view. –
She glanced at it but lightly,
        And I knew
That one from him that day had reached her too.

There was no time for scruple;
        Secretly
I filched her missive, conned it,
        Learnt that he
Would lodge with her ere he came home to me.

To reach the port before her,
        And, unscanned,
There wait to intercept them
        Soon I planned:
That, in her stead, *I* might before him stand.

So purposed, so effected;
        At the inn
Assigned, I found her hidden: –
        O that sin
Should bear what she bore when I entered in!

Her heavy lids grew laden
        With despairs,
Her lips made soundless movements
        Unawares,
While I peered at the chamber hired as theirs.

And as beside its doorway,
 Deadly hued,
One inside, one withoutside
 We two stood,
He came – my husband – as she knew he would.

No pleasurable triumph
 Was that sight!
The ghastly disappointment
 Broke them quite.
What love was theirs, to move them with such might!

'Madam, forgive me!' said she,
 Sorrow bent,
'A child – I soon shall bear him. . . .
 Yes – I meant
To tell you – that he won me ere he went.'

Then, as it were, within me
 Something snapped,
As if my soul had largened:
 Conscience-capped,
I saw myself the snarer – them the trapped.

'My hate dies, and I promise,
 Grace-beguiled,'
I said, 'to care for you, be
 Reconciled;
And cherish, and take interest in the child.'

Without more words I pressed him
 Through the door
Within which she stood, powerless
 To say more,
And closed it on them, and downstairward bore.

'He joins his wife – my sister,'
 I, below,
Remarked in going – lightly –
 Even as though
All had come right, and we had arranged it so. . . .

As I, my road retracing,
    Left them free,
The night alone embracing
    Childless me,
I held I had not stirred God wrothfully.

The Roman Road

The Roman Road runs straight and bare
As the pale parting-line in hair
Across the heath. And thoughtful men
Contrast its days of Now and Then,
And delve, and measure, and compare;
Visioning on the vacant air
Helmed legionaries, who proudly rear
The Eagle, as they pace again
                The Roman Road.

But no tall brass-helmed legionnaire
Haunts it for me. Uprises there
A mother's form upon my ken,
Guiding my infant steps, as when
We walked that ancient thoroughfare,
                The Roman Road.

The Reminder

While I watch the Christmas blaze
Paint the room with ruddy rays,
Something makes my vision glide
To the frosty scene outside.

There, to reach a rotting berry,
Toils a thrush, – constrained to very
Dregs of food by sharp distress,
Taking such with thankfulness.

Why, O starving bird, when I
One day's joy would justify,
And put misery out of view,
Do you make me notice you!

Night in the Old Home

When the wasting embers redden the chimney-breast,
And Life's bare pathway looms like a desert track to me,
And from hall and parlour the living have gone to their rest,
My perished people who housed them here come back to me.

They come and seat them around in their mouldy places,
Now and then bending towards me a glance of wistfulness,
A strange upbraiding smile upon all their faces,
And in the bearing of each a passive tristfulness.

'Do you uphold me, lingering and languishing here,
A pale late plant of your once strong stock?' I say to them;
'A thinker of crooked thoughts upon Life in the sere,
And on That which consigns men to night after showing the day to
        them?'

' – O let be the Wherefore! We fevered our years not thus:
Take of Life what it grants, without question!' they answer me
        seemingly.
'Enjoy, suffer, wait: spread the table here freely like us,
And, satisfied, placid, unfretting, watch Time away beamingly!'

After the Last Breath

(J.H. 1813–1904)*

There's no more to be done, or feared, or hoped;
None now need watch, speak low, and list, and tire;
No irksome crease outsmoothed, no pillow sloped
        Does she require.

Blankly we gaze. We are free to go or stay;
Our morrow's anxious plans have missed their aim;
Whether we leave to-night or wait till day
        Counts as the same.

The lettered vessels of medicaments
Seem asking wherefore we have set them here;
Each palliative its silly face presents
    As useless gear.

And yet we feel that something savours well;
We note a numb relief withheld before;
Our well-beloved is prisoner in the cell
    Of Time no more.

We see by littles now the deft achievement
Whereby she has escaped the Wrongers all,
In view of which our momentary bereavement
    Outshapes but small.

1904

The Dear

I plodded to Fairmile Hill-top, where
    A maiden one fain would guard
From every hazard and every care
    Advanced on the roadside sward.

I wondered how succeeding suns
    Would shape her wayfarings,
And wished some Power might take such ones
    Under Its warding wings.

The busy breeze came up the hill
    And smartened her cheek to red,
And frizzled her hair to a haze. With a will
    'Good-morning, my Dear!' I said.

She glanced from me to the far-off gray,
    And, with proud severity,
'Good-morning to you – though I may say
    I am not *your* Dear,' quoth she:

'For I am the Dear of one not here –
    One far from his native land!' –
And she passed me by; and I did not try
    To make her understand.

1901

One We Knew

(M.H. *1772–1857*)

She told how they used to form for the country dances –
    'The Triumph', 'The New-rigged Ship' –
To the light of the guttering wax in the panelled manses,
    And in cots to the blink of a dip.

She spoke of the wild 'poussetting' and 'allemanding'
    On carpet, on oak, and on sod;
And the two long rows of ladies and gentlemen standing,
    And the figures the couples trod.

She showed us the spot where the maypole was yearly planted,
    And where the bandsmen stood
While breeched and kerchiefed partners whirled, and panted
    To choose each other for good.

She told of that far-back day when they learnt astounded
    Of the death of the King of France:
Of the Terror; and then of Bonaparte's unbounded
    Ambition and arrogance.

Of how his threats woke warlike preparations
    Along the southern strand,
And how each night brought tremors and trepidations
    Lest morning should see him land.

She said she had often heard the gibbet creaking
    As it swayed in the lightning flash,
Had caught from the neighbouring town a small child's shrieking
    At the cart-tail under the lash. . . .

With cap-framed face and long gaze into the embers –
    We seated around her knees –
She would dwell on such dead themes, not as one who remembers,
    But rather as one who sees.

She seemed one left behind of a band gone distant
    So far that no tongue could hail:
Past things retold were to her as things existent,
    Things present but as a tale.

20 May 1902

The Unborn*

I rose at night, and visited
    The Cave of the Unborn:
And crowding shapes surrounded me
For tidings of the life to be,
Who long had prayed the silent Head
    To haste its advent morn.

Their eyes were lit with artless trust,
    Hope thrilled their every tone;
'A scene the loveliest, is it not?
A pure delight, a beauty-spot
Where all is gentle, true and just,
    And darkness is unknown?'

My heart was anguished for their sake,
    I could not frame a word;
And they descried my sunken face,
And seemed to read therein, and trace
The news that pity would not break,
    Nor truth leave unaverred.

And as I silently retired
    I turned and watched them still,
And they came helter-skelter out,
Driven forward like a rabble rout

Into the world they had so desired,
By the all-immanent Will.

1905

The Man He Killed

'Had he and I but met
By some old ancient inn,
We should have sat us down to wet
Right many a nipperkin!

'But ranged as infantry,
And staring face to face,
I shot at him as he at me,
And killed him in his place.

'I shot him dead because –
Because he was my foe,
Just so: my foe of course he was;
That's clear enough; although

'He thought he'd 'list, perhaps,
Off-hand like – just as I –
Was out of work – had sold his traps –
No other reason why.

'Yes; quaint and curious war is!
You shoot a fellow down
You'd treat if met where any bar is,
Or help to half-a-crown.'

1902

from

SATIRES OF CIRCUMSTANCE: LYRICS AND REVERIES

In Front of the Landscape

Plunging and labouring on in a tide of visions,
    Dolorous and dear,
Forward I pushed my way as amid waste waters
    Stretching around,
Through whose eddies there glimmered the customed landscape
    Yonder and near

Blotted to feeble mist. And the coomb and the upland
    Coppice-crowned,
Ancient chalk-pit, milestone, rills in the grass-flat
    Stroked by the light,
Seemed but a ghost-like gauze, and no substantial
    Meadow or mound.

What were the infinite spectacles featuring foremost
    Under my sight,
Hindering me to discern my paced advancement
    Lengthening to miles;
What were the re-creations killing the daytime
    As by the night?

O they were speechful faces, gazing insistent,
    Some as with smiles,
Some as with slow-born tears that brinily trundled
    Over the wrecked
Cheeks that were fair in their flush-time, ash now with anguish,
    Harrowed by wiles.

Yes, I could see them, feel them, hear them, address them –
    Halo-bedecked –
And, alas, onwards, shaken by fierce unreason,
    Rigid in hate,
Smitten by years-long wryness born of misprision,
    Dreaded, suspect.

Then there would breast me shining sights, sweet seasons
    Further in date;
Instruments of strings with the tenderest passion
    Vibrant, beside
Lamps long extinguished, robes, cheeks, eyes with the earth's crust
    Now corporate.

Also there rose a headland of hoary aspect
    Gnawed by the tide,
Frilled by the nimb of the morning as two friends stood there
    Guilelessly glad –
Wherefore they knew not – touched by the fringe of an ecstasy
    Scantly descried.

Later images too did the day unfurl me,
    Shadowed and sad,
Clay cadavers of those who had shared in the dramas,
    Laid now at ease,
Passions all spent, chiefest the one of the broad brow
    Sepulture-clad.

So did beset me scenes, miscalled of the bygone,
    Over the leaze,
Past the clump, and down to where lay the beheld ones;
    – Yea, as the rhyme
Sung by the sea-swell, so in their pleading dumbness
    Captured me these.

For, their lost revisiting manifestations
    In their live time
Much had I slighted, caring not for their purport,
    Seeing behind
Things more coveted, reckoned the better worth calling
    Sweet, sad, sublime.

Thus do they now show hourly before the intenser
    Stare of the mind
As they were ghosts avenging their slights by my bypast
    Body-borne eyes,
Show, too, with fuller translation than rested upon them
    As living kind.

Hence wag the tongues of the passing people, saying
    In their surmise,
'Ah – whose is this dull form that perambulates, seeing nought
    Round him that looms
Whithersoever his footsteps turn in his farings,
    Save a few tombs?'

Channel Firing*

That night your great guns, unawares,
Shook all our coffins as we lay,
And broke the chancel window-squares,
We thought it was the Judgment-day

And sat upright. While drearisome
Arose the howl of wakened hounds:
The mouse let fall the altar-crumb,
The worms drew back into the mounds,

The glebe cow drooled. Till God called, 'No;
It's gunnery practice out at sea
Just as before you went below;
The world is as it used to be:

'All nations striving strong to make
Red war yet redder. Mad as hatters
They do no more for Christés sake
Than you who are helpless in such matters.

'That this is not the judgment-hour
For some of them's a blessed thing,
For if it were they'd have to scour
Hell's floor for so much threatening. . . .

'Ha, ha. It will be warmer when
I blow the trumpet (if indeed
I ever do; for you are men,
And rest eternal sorely need).'

So down we lay again. 'I wonder,
Will the world ever saner be,'
Said one, 'than when He sent us under
In our indifferent century!'

And many a skeleton shook his head.
'Instead of preaching forty year,'
My neighbour Parson Thirdly said,
'I wish I had stuck to pipes and beer.'

Again the guns disturbed the hour,
Roaring their readiness to avenge,
As far inland as Stourton Tower,
And Camelot, and starlit Stonehenge.

April 1914

The Convergence of the Twain*

(*Lines on the loss of the 'Titanic'*)

i

In a solitude of the sea
Deep from human vanity,
And the Pride of Life that planned her, stilly couches she.

ii

Steel chambers, late the pyres
Of her salamandrine fires,
Cold currents thrid, and turn to rhythmic tidal lyres.

iii

Over the mirrors meant
To glass the opulent
The sea-worm crawls – grotesque, slimed, dumb, indifferent.

iv

Jewels in joy designed
To ravish the sensuous mind
Lie lightless, all their sparkles bleared and black and blind.

v

Dim moon-eyed fishes near
Gaze at the gilded gear
And query: 'What does this vaingloriousness down here?'...

vi

Well: while was fashioning
This creature of cleaving wing,
The Immanent Will that stirs and urges everything

vii

Prepared a sinister mate
For her — so gaily great —
A Shape of Ice, for the time far and dissociate.

viii

And as the smart ship grew
In stature, grace, and hue,
In shadowy silent distance grew the Iceberg too.

ix

Alien they seemed to be:
No mortal eye could see
The intimate welding of their later history,

x

Or sign that they were bent
By paths coincident
On being anon twin halves of one august event,

xi

Till the Spinner of the Years
Said 'Now!' And each one hears,
And consummation comes, and jars two hemispheres.

After the Visit

(To F.E.D.)

Come again to the place
Where your presence was as a leaf that skims
Down a drouthy way whose ascent bedims
The bloom on the farer's face.

Come again, with the feet
That were light on the green as a thistledown ball,
And those mute ministrations to one and to all
        Beyond a man's saying sweet.

Until then the faint scent
Of the bordering flowers swam unheeded away,
And I marked not the charm in the changes of day
        As the cloud-colours came and went.

Through the dark corridors
Your walk was so soundless I did not know
Your form from a phantom's of long ago
        Said to pass on the ancient floors,

Till you drew from the shade,
And I saw the large luminous living eyes
Regard me in fixed inquiring-wise
        As those of a soul that weighed,

Scarce consciously,
The eternal question of what Life was,
And why we were there, and by whose strange laws
        That which mattered most could not be.

When I Set Out for Lyonnesse*

(1870)

When I set out for Lyonnesse,
        A hundred miles away,
        The rime was on the spray,
And starlight lit my lonesomeness
When I set out for Lyonnesse
        A hundred miles away.

What would bechance at Lyonnesse
        While I should sojourn there
        No prophet durst declare,

Nor did the wisest wizard guess
What would bechance at Lyonnesse
    While I should sojourn there.

When I came back from Lyonnesse
    With magic in my eyes,
        All marked with mute surmise
My radiance rare and fathomless,
When I came back from Lyonnesse
    With magic in my eyes!

A Thunderstorm in Town

(A Reminiscence: 1893)

She wore a new 'terra-cotta' dress,
And we stayed, because of the pelting storm,
Within the hansom's dry recess,
Though the horse had stopped; yea, motionless
    We sat on, snug and warm.

Then the downpour ceased, to my sharp sad pain,
And the glass that had screened our forms before
Flew up, and out she sprang to her door:
I should have kissed her if the rain
    Had lasted a minute more.

Beyond the Last Lamp*

(Near Tooting Common)

i

While rain, with eve in partnership,
Descended darkly, drip, drip, drip,
Beyond the last lone lamp I passed
    Walking slowly, whispering sadly,
        Two linked loiterers, wan, downcast:
Some heavy thought constrained each face,
And blinded them to time and place.

ii

The pair seemed lovers, yet absorbed
In mental scenes no longer orbed
By love's young rays. Each countenance
　　As it slowly, as it sadly
　　Caught the lamplight's yellow glance,
Held in suspense a misery
At things which had been or might be.

iii

When I retrod that watery way
Some hours beyond the droop of day,
Still I found pacing there the twain
　　Just as slowly, just as sadly,
　　Heedless of the night and rain.
One could but wonder who they were
And what wild woe detained them there.

iv

Though thirty years of blur and blot
Have slid since I beheld that spot,
And saw in curious converse there
　　Moving slowly, moving sadly
　　That mysterious tragic pair,
Its olden look may linger on –
All but the couple; they have gone.

v

Whither? Who knows, indeed. . . . And yet
To me, when nights are weird and wet,
Without those comrades there at tryst
　　Creeping slowly, creeping sadly,
　　That lone lane does not exist.
There they seem brooding on their pain,
And will, while such a lane remain.

My Spirit Will Not Haunt the Mound

My spirit will not haunt the mound
        Above my breast,
But travel, memory-possessed,
To where my tremulous being found
        Life largest, best.

My phantom-footed shape will go
        When nightfall grays
Hither and thither along the ways
I and another used to know
        In backward days.

And there you'll find me, if a jot
        You still should care
For me, and for my curious air;
If otherwise, then I shall not,
        For you, be there.

Wessex Heights

(1896)

There are some heights in Wessex, shaped as if by a kindly hand
For thinking, dreaming, dying on, and at crises when I stand,
Say, on Ingpen Beacon eastward, or on Wylls-Neck westwardly,
I seem where I was before my birth, and after death may be.

In the lowlands I have no comrade, not even the lone man's
        friend —
Her who suffereth long and is kind; accepts what he is too weak to
        mend:
Down there they are dubious and askance; there nobody thinks as I,
But mind-chains do not clank where one's next neighbour is the sky.

In the towns I am tracked by phantoms having weird detective
        ways —
Shadows of beings who fellowed with myself of earlier days:
They hang about at places, and they say harsh heavy things —
Men with a wintry sneer, and women with tart disparagings.

Down there I seem to be false to myself, my simple self that was,
And is not now, and I see him watching, wondering what crass
    cause
Can have merged him into such a strange continuator as this,
Who yet has something in common with himself, my chrysalis.

I cannot go to the great grey Plain; there's a figure against the
    moon,
Nobody sees it but I, and it makes my breast beat out of tune;
I cannot go to the tall-spired town, being barred by the forms now
    passed
For everybody but me, in whose long vision they stand there fast.

There's a ghost at Yell'ham Bottom chiding loud at the fall of the
    night,
There's a ghost in Froom-side Vale, thin-lipped and vague, in a
    shroud of white,
There is one in the railway train whenever I do not want it near,
I see its profile against the pane, saying what I would not hear.

As for one rare fair woman, I am now but a thought of hers,
I enter her mind and another thought succeeds me that she prefers;
Yet my love for her in its fulness she herself even did not know;
Well, time cures hearts of tenderness, and now I can let her go.

So I am found on Ingpen Beacon, or on Wylls-Neck to the west,
Or else on homely Bulbarrow, or little Pilsdon Crest,
Where men have never cared to haunt, nor women have walked
    with me,
And ghosts then keep their distance; and I know some liberty.

The Place on the Map*

i

I look upon the map that hangs by me –
Its shires and towns and rivers lined in varnished artistry –
    And I mark a jutting height
   Coloured purple, with a margin of blue sea.

ii

— 'Twas a day of latter summer, hot and dry;
Ay, even the waves seemed drying as we walked on, she and I,
   By this spot where, calmly quite,
She unfolded what would happen by and by.

iii

This hanging map depicts the coast and place,
And re-creates therewith our unforeboded troublous case
   All distinctly to my sight,
And her tension, and the aspect of her face.

iv

Weeks and weeks we had loved beneath that blazing blue,
Which had lost the art of raining, as her eyes to-day had too,
   While she told what, as by sleight,
Shot our firmament with rays of ruddy hue.

v

For the wonder and the wormwood of the whole
Was that what in realms of reason would have joyed our double
      soul
   Wore a torrid tragic light
Under order-keeping's rigorous control.

vi

So, the map revives her words, the spot, the time,
And the thing we found we had to face before the next year's
      prime;
   The charted coast stares bright,
And its episode comes back in pantomime.

God's Funeral*

i

   I saw a slowly-stepping train —
Lined on the brows, scoop-eyed and bent and hoar —
Following in files across a twilit plain
A strange and mystic form the foremost bore.

ii

And by contagious throbs of thought
Or latent knowledge that within me lay
And had already stirred me, I was wrought
To consciousness of sorrow even as they.

iii

The fore-borne shape, to my blurred eyes,
At first seemed man-like, and anon to change
To an amorphous cloud of marvellous size,
At times endowed with wings of glorious range.

iv

And this phantasmal variousness
Ever possessed it as they drew along:
Yet throughout all it symboled none the less
Potency vast and loving-kindness strong.

v

Almost before I knew I bent
Towards the moving columns without a word;
They, growing in bulk and numbers as they went,
Struck out sick thoughts that could be overheard: —

vi

'O man-projected Figure, of late
Imaged as we, thy knell who shall survive?
Whence came it we were tempted to create
One whom we can no longer keep alive?

vii

'Framing him jealous, fierce, at first,
We gave him justice as the ages rolled,
Will to bless those by circumstance accurst,
And longsuffering, and mercies manifold.

viii

'And, tricked by our own early dream
And need of solace, we grew self-deceived,
Our making soon our maker did we deem,
And what we had imagined we believed.

ix

'Till, in Time's stayless stealthy swing,
Uncompromising rude reality
Mangled the Monarch of our fashioning,
Who quavered, sank; and now has ceased to be.

x

'So, toward our myth's oblivion,
Darkling, and languid-lipped, we creep and grope
Sadlier than those who wept in Babylon,
Whose Zion was a still abiding hope.

xi

'How sweet it was in years far hied
To start the wheels of day with trustful prayer,
To lie down liegely at the eventide
And feel a blest assurance he was there!

xii

'And who or what shall fill his place?
Whither will wanderers turn distracted eyes
For some fixed star to stimulate their pace
Towards the goal of their enterprise?'...

xiii

Some in the background then I saw,
Sweet women, youths, men, all incredulous,
Who chimed: 'This is a counterfeit of straw,
This requiem mockery! Still he lives to us!'

xiv

I could not buoy their faith: and yet
Many I had known: with all I sympathized;
And though struck speechless, I did not forget
That what was mourned for, I, too, long had prized.

xv

Still, how to bear such loss I deemed
The insistent question for each animate mind,
And gazing, to my growing sight there seemed
A pale yet positive gleam low down behind,

xvi

Whereof, to lift the general night,
A certain few who stood aloof had said,
'See you upon the horizon that small light –
Swelling somewhat?' Each mourner shook his head.

xvii

And they composed a crowd of whom
Some were right good, and many nigh the best. . . .
Thus dazed and puzzled 'twixt the gleam and gloom
Mechanically I followed with the rest.

1908–10

The Discovery

I wandered to a crude coast
    Like a ghost;
Upon the hills I saw fires –
    Funeral pyres
Seemingly – and heard breaking
Waves like distant cannonades that set the land shaking.

And so I never once guessed
    A Love-nest,
Bowered and candle-lit, lay
    In my way,
Till I found a hid hollow,
Where I burst on her my heart could not but follow.

The Year's Awakening

How do you know that the pilgrim track
Along the belting zodiac
Swept by the sun in his seeming rounds
Is traced by now to the Fishes' bounds
And into the Ram, when weeks of cloud
Have wrapt the sky in a clammy shroud,
And never as yet a tint of spring

Has shown in the Earth's apparelling;
    O vespering bird, how do you know,
        How do you know?

How do you know, deep underground,
Hid in your bed from sight and sound,
Without a turn in temperature,
With weather life can scarce endure,
That light has won a fraction's strength,
And day put on some moments' length,
Whereof in merest rote will come,
Weeks hence, mild airs that do not numb;
    O crocus root, how do you know,
        How do you know?

February 1910

Under the Waterfall

'Whenever I plunge my arm, like this,
In a basin of water, I never miss
The sweet sharp sense of a fugitive day
Fetched back from its thickening shroud of gray.
    Hence the only prime
    And real love-rhyme
    That I know by heart,
    And that leaves no smart,
Is the purl of a little valley fall
About three spans wide and two spans tall
Over a table of solid rock,
And into a scoop of the self-same block;
The purl of a runlet that never ceases
In stir of kingdoms, in wars, in peaces;
With a hollow boiling voice it speaks
And has spoken since hills were turfless peaks.'

'And why gives this the only prime
Idea to you of a real love-rhyme?
And why does plunging your arm in a bowl
Full of spring water, bring throbs to your soul?'

'Well, under the fall, in a crease of the stone,
Though where precisely none ever has known,
Jammed darkly, nothing to show how prized,
And by now with its smoothness opalized,
     Is a drinking-glass:
     For, down that pass
     My lover and I
     Walked under a sky
Of blue with a leaf-wove awning of green,
In the burn of August, to paint the scene,
And we placed our basket of fruit and wine
By the runlet's rim, where we sat to dine;
And when we had drunk from the glass together,
Arched by the oak-copse from the weather,
I held the vessel to rinse in the fall,
Where it slipped, and sank, and was past recall,
Though we stooped and plumbed the little abyss
With long bared arms. There the glass still is.
And, as said, if I thrust my arm below
Cold water in basin or bowl, a throe
From the past awakens a sense of that time,
And the glass we used, and the cascade's rhyme.
The basin seems the pool, and its edge
The hard smooth face of the brook-side ledge,
And the leafy pattern of china-ware
The hanging plants that were bathing there.

'By night, by day, when it shines or lours,
There lies intact that chalice of ours,
And its presence adds to the rhyme of love
Persistently sung by the fall above.
No lip has touched it since his and mine
In turns therefrom sipped lovers' wine.'

The Going

Why did you give no hint that night
That quickly after the morrow's dawn,
And calmly, as if indifferent quite,
You would close your term here, up and be gone
    Where I could not follow
    With wing of swallow
To gain one glimpse of you ever anon!

    Never to bid good-bye,
    Or lip me the softest call,
Or utter a wish for a word, while I
Saw morning harden upon the wall,
    Unmoved, unknowing
    That your great going
Had place that moment, and altered all.

Why do you make me leave the house
And think for a breath it is you I see
At the end of the alley of bending boughs
Where so often at dusk you used to be;
    Till in darkening dankness
    The yawning blankness
Of the perspective sickens me!

    You were she who abode
    By those red-veined rocks far West,
You were the swan-necked one who rode
Along the beetling Beeny Crest,
    And, reining nigh me,
    Would muse and eye me,
While Life unrolled us its very best.

Why, then, latterly did we not speak,
Did we not think of those days long dead,

And ere your vanishing strive to seek
That time's renewal? We might have said,
    'In this bright spring weather
    We'll visit together
Those places that once we visited.'

    Well, well! All's past amend,
    Unchangeable. It must go.
I seem but a dead man held on end
To sink down soon. . . . O you could not know
    That such swift fleeing
    No soul foreseeing –
Not even I – would undo me so!

December 1912

Your Last Drive

Here by the moorway you returned,
And saw the borough lights ahead
That lit your face – all undiscerned
To be in a week the face of the dead,
And you told of the charm of that haloed view
That never again would beam on you.

And on your left you passed the spot
Where eight days later you were to lie,
And be spoken of as one who was not;
Beholding it with a heedless eye
As alien from you, though under its tree
You soon would halt everlastingly.

I drove not with you. . . . Yet had I sat
At your side that eve I should not have seen
That the countenance I was glancing at
Had a last-time look in the flickering sheen,
Nor have read the writing upon your face,
'I go hence soon to my resting-place;

'You may miss me then. But I shall not know
How many times you visit me there,

Or what your thoughts are, or if you go
There never at all. And I shall not care.
Should you censure me I shall take no heed,
And even your praises no more shall need.'

True: never you'll know. And you will not mind.
But shall I then slight you because of such?
Dear ghost, in the past did you ever find
The thought 'What profit,' move me much?
Yet abides the fact, indeed, the same, —
You are past love, praise, indifference, blame.

December 1912

The Walk

You did not walk with me
Of late to the hill-top tree
        By the gated ways,
        As in earlier days;
        You were weak and lame,
        So you never came,
And I went alone, and I did not mind,
Not thinking of you as left behind.

I walked up there to-day
Just in the former way;
        Surveyed around
        The familiar ground
        By myself again:
        What difference, then?
Only that underlying sense
Of the look of a room on returning thence.

Rain on a Grave

Clouds spout upon her
        Their waters amain
        In ruthless disdain, —

Her who but lately
   Had shivered with pain
As at touch of dishonour
If there had lit on her
So coldly, so straightly
   Such arrows of rain:

One who to shelter
   Her delicate head
Would quicken and quicken
   Each tentative tread
If drops chanced to pelt her
   That summertime spills
   In dust-paven rills
When thunder-clouds thicken
   And birds close their bills.

Would that I lay there
   And she were housed here!
Or better, together
Were folded away there
Exposed to one weather
We both, – who would stray there
When sunny the day there,
   Or evening was clear
   At the prime of the year.

Soon will be growing
   Green blades from her mound,
And daisies be showing
   Like stars on the ground,
Till she form part of them –
Ay – the sweet heart of them,
Loved beyond measure
With a child's pleasure
   All her life's round.

31 January 1913

I Found Her Out There*

I found her out there
On a slope few see,
That falls westwardly
To the salt-edged air,
Where the ocean breaks
On the purple strand,
And the hurricane shakes
The solid land.

I brought her here,
And have laid her to rest
In a noiseless nest
No sea beats near.
She will never be stirred
In her loamy cell
By the waves long heard
And loved so well.

So she does not sleep
By those haunted heights
The Atlantic smites
And the blind gales sweep,
Whence she often would gaze
At Dundagel's famed head,
While the dipping blaze
Dyed her face fire-red;

And would sigh at the tale
Of sunk Lyonnesse,
As a wind-tugged tress
Flapped her cheek like a flail;
Or listen at whiles
With a thought-bound brow
To the murmuring miles
She is far from now.

Yet her shade, maybe,
Will creep underground
Till it catch the sound

Of that western sea
As it swells and sobs
Where she once domiciled,
And joy in its throbs
With the heart of a child.

Without Ceremony

It was your way, my dear,
To vanish without a word
When callers, friends, or kin
Had left, and I hastened in
To rejoin you, as I inferred.

And when you'd a mind to career
Off anywhere – say to town –
You were all on a sudden gone
Before I had thought thereon,
Or noticed your trunks were down.

So, now that you disappear
For ever in that swift style,
Your meaning seems to me
Just as it used to be:
'Good-bye is not worth while!'

Lament

How she would have loved
A party to-day! –
Bright-hatted and gloved,
With table and tray
And chairs on the lawn
Her smiles would have shone
With welcomings. . . . But
She is shut, she is shut
        From friendship's spell
        In the jailing shell
        Of her tiny cell.

Or she would have reigned
At a dinner to-night
With ardours unfeigned,
And a generous delight;
All in her abode
She'd have freely bestowed
On her guests. . . . But alas,
She is shut under grass
 Where no cups flow,
 Powerless to know
 That it might be so.

And she would have sought
With a child's eager glance
The shy snowdrops brought
By the new year's advance,
And peered in the rime
Of Candlemas-time
For crocuses . . . chanced
It that she were not tranced
 From sights she loved best;
 Wholly possessed
 By an infinite rest!

And we are here staying
Amid these stale things,
Who care not for gaying,
And those junketings
That used so to joy her,
And never to cloy her
As us they cloy! . . . But
She is shut, she is shut
 From the cheer of them, dead
 To all done and said
 In her yew-arched bed.

The Haunter

He does not think that I haunt here nightly:
    How shall I let him know
That whither his fancy sets him wandering
    I, too, alertly go? —
Hover and hover a few feet from him
    Just as I used to do,
But cannot answer the words he lifts me —
    Only listen thereto!

When I could answer he did not say them:
    When I could let him know
How I would like to join in his journeys
    Seldom he wished to go.
Now that he goes and wants me with him
    More than he used to do,
Never he sees my faithful phantom
    Though he speaks thereto.

Yes, I companion him to places
    Only dreamers know,
Where the shy hares print long paces,
    Where the night rooks go;
Into old aisles where the past is all to him,
    Close as his shade can do,
Always lacking the power to call to him,
    Near as I reach thereto!

What a good haunter I am, O tell him!
    Quickly make him know
If he but sigh since my loss befell him
    Straight to his side I go.
Tell him a faithful one is doing
    All that love can do
Still that his path may be worth pursuing,
    And to bring peace thereto.

The Voice

Woman much missed, how you call to me, call to me,
Saying that now you are not as you were
When you had changed from the one who was all to me,
But as at first, when our day was fair.

Can it be you that I hear? Let me view you, then,
Standing as when I drew near to the town
Where you would wait for me: yes, as I knew you then,
Even to the original air-blue gown!

Or is it only the breeze, in its listlessness
Travelling across the wet mead to me here,
You being ever dissolved to wan wistlessness,
Heard no more again far or near?

    Thus I; faltering forward,
    Leaves around me falling,
Wind oozing thin through the thorn from norward,
    And the woman calling.

December 1912

His Visitor

I come across from Mellstock while the moon wastes weaker
To behold where I lived with you for twenty years and more:
I shall go in the gray, at the passing of the mail-train,
And need no setting open of the long familiar door
    As before.

The change I notice in my once own quarters!
A formal-fashioned border where the daisies used to be,
The rooms new painted, and the pictures altered,
And other cups and saucers, and no cosy nook for tea
    As with me.

I discern the dim faces of the sleep-wrapt servants;
They are not those who tended me through feeble hours and
      strong,

But strangers quite, who never knew my rule here,
Who never saw me painting, never heard my softling song
              Float along.

So I don't want to linger in this re-decked dwelling,
I feel too uneasy at the contrasts I behold,
And I make again for Mellstock to return here never,
And rejoin the roomy silence, and the mute and manifold
              Souls of old.

1913

A Circular

As 'legal representative'
I read a missive not my own,
On new designs the senders give
        For clothes, in tints as shown.

Here figure blouses, gowns for tea,
And presentation-trains of state,
Charming ball-dresses, millinery,
        Warranted up to date.

And this gay-pictured, spring-time shout
Of Fashion, hails what lady proud?
Her who before last year ebbed out
        Was costumed in a shroud.

A Dream or No

Why go to Saint-Juliot? What's Juliot to me?
        Some strange necromancy
        But charmed me to fancy
That much of my life claims the spot as its key.

Yes. I have had dreams of that place in the West,
        And a maiden abiding
        Thereat as in hiding;
Fair-eyed and white-shouldered, broad-browed and brown-tressed.

And of how, coastward bound on a night long ago,
      There lonely I found her,
      The sea-birds around her,
And other than nigh things uncaring to know.

So sweet her life there (in my thought has it seemed)
      That quickly she drew me
      To take her unto me,
And lodge her long years with me. Such have I dreamed.

But nought of that maid from Saint-Juliot I see;
      Can she ever have been here,
      And shed her life's sheen here,
The woman I thought a long housemate with me?

Does there even a place like Saint-Juliot exist?
      Or a Vallency Valley
      With stream and leafed alley,
Or Beeny, or Bos with its flounce flinging mist?

February 1913

After a Journey

Hereto I come to view a voiceless ghost;
   Whither, O whither will its whim now draw me?
Up the cliff, down, till I'm lonely, lost,
   And the unseen waters' ejaculations awe me.
Where you will next be there's no knowing,
   Facing round about me everywhere,
      With your nut-coloured hair,
And gray eyes, and rose-flush coming and going.

Yes: I have re-entered your olden haunts at last;
   Through the years, through the dead scenes I have tracked you;
What have you now found to say of our past –
   Scanned across the dark space wherein I have lacked you?
Summer gave us sweets, but autumn wrought division?
   Things were not lastly as firstly well
      With us twain, you tell?
But all's closed now, despite Time's derision.

I see what you are doing: you are leading me on
   To the spots we knew when we haunted here together,
The waterfall, above which the mist-bow shone
   At the then fair hour in the then fair weather,
And the cave just under, with a voice still so hollow
   That it seems to call out to me from forty years ago,
     When you were all aglow,
And not the thin ghost that I now fraily follow!

Ignorant of what there is flitting here to see,
   The waked birds preen and the seals flop lazily;
Soon you will have, Dear, to vanish from me,
   For the stars close their shutters and the dawn whitens hazily.
Trust me, I mind not, though Life lours,
   The bringing me here; nay, bring me here again!
     I am just the same as when
Our days were a joy, and our paths through flowers.

Pentargan Bay

A Death-Day Recalled

Beeny did not quiver,
   Juliot grew not gray,
Thin Vallency's river
   Held its wonted way.
Bos seemed not to utter
   Dimmest note of dirge,
Targan mouth a mutter
   To its creamy surge.

Yet though these, unheeding,
   Listless, passed the hour
Of her spirit's speeding,
   She had, in her flower,
Sought and loved the places —
   Much and often pined
For their lonely faces
   When in towns confined.

Why did not Vallency
    In his purl deplore
One whose haunts were whence he
    Drew his limpid store?
Why did Bos not thunder,
    Targan apprehend
Body and Breath were sunder
    Of their former friend?

Beeny Cliff*

March 1870–March 1913

i

O the opal and the sapphire of that wandering western sea,
And the woman riding high above with bright hair flapping free –
The woman whom I loved so, and who loyally loved me.

ii

The pale mews plained below us, and the waves seemed far away
In a nether sky, engrossed in saying their ceaseless babbling say,
As we laughed light-heartedly aloft on that clear-sunned March
    day.

iii

A little cloud then cloaked us, and there flew an irised rain,
And the Atlantic dyed its levels with a dull misfeatured stain,
And then the sun burst out again, and purples prinked the main.

iv

– Still in all its chasmal beauty bulks old Beeny to the sky,
And shall she and I not go there once again now March is nigh,
And the sweet things said in that March say anew there by and by?

v

What if still in chasmal beauty looms that wild weird western
    shore,
The woman now is – elsewhere – whom the ambling pony bore,
And nor knows nor cares for Beeny, and will laugh there
    nevermore.

At Castle Boterel

As I drive to the junction of lane and highway,
    And the drizzle bedrenches the waggonette,
I look behind at the fading byway,
    And see on its slope, now glistening wet,
        Distinctly yet

Myself and a girlish form benighted
    In dry March weather. We climb the road
Beside a chaise. We had just alighted
    To ease the sturdy pony's load
        When he sighed and slowed.

What we did as we climbed, and what we talked of
    Matters not much, nor to what it led, —
Something that life will not be balked of
    Without rude reason till hope is dead,
        And feeling fled.

It filled but a minute. But was there ever
    A time of such quality, since or before,
In that hill's story? To one mind never,
    Though it has been climbed, foot-swift, foot-sore,
        By thousands more.

Primaeval rocks form the road's steep border,
    And much have they faced there, first and last,
Of the transitory in Earth's long order;
    But what they record in colour and cast
        Is — that we two passed.

And to me, though Time's unflinching rigour,
    In mindless rote, has ruled from sight
The substance now, one phantom figure
    Remains on the slope, as when that night
        Saw us alight.

I look and see it there, shrinking, shrinking,
    I look back at it amid the rain

For the very last time; for my sand is sinking,
  And I shall traverse old love's domain
    Never again.

March 1913

Places

Nobody says: Ah, that is the place
Where chanced, in the hollow of years ago,
What none of the Three Towns cared to know –
The birth of a little girl of grace –
The sweetest the house saw, first or last;
    Yet it was so
    On that day long past.

Nobody thinks: There, there she lay
In a room by the Hoe, like the bud of a flower,
And listened, just after the bedtime hour,
To the stammering chimes that used to play
The quaint Old Hundred-and-Thirteenth tune
    In Saint Andrew's tower
    Night, morn, and noon.

Nobody calls to mind that here
Upon Boterel Hill, where the waggoners skid,
With cheeks whose airy flush outbid
Fresh fruit in bloom, and free of fear,
She cantered down, as if she must fall
    (Though she never did),
    To the charm of all.

Nay: one there is to whom these things,
That nobody else's mind calls back,
Have a savour that scenes in being lack,
And a presence more than the actual brings;
To whom to-day is beneaped and stale,
    And its urgent clack
    But a vapid tale.

Plymouth, March 1913

The Phantom Horsewoman

i

Queer are the ways of a man I know:
        He comes and stands
        In a careworn craze,
        And looks at the sands
        And the seaward haze
        With moveless hands
        And face and gaze,
        Then turns to go . . .
And what does he see when he gazes so?

ii

They say he sees as an instant thing
        More clear than to-day,
        A sweet soft scene
        That was once in play
        By that briny green;
        Yes, notes alway
        Warm, real, and keen,
        What his back years bring —
A phantom of his own figuring.

iii

Of this vision of his they might say more:
        Not only there
        Does he see this sight,
        But everywhere
        In his brain — day, night,
        As if on the air
        It were drawn rose bright —
        Yea, far from that shore
Does he carry this vision of heretofore:

iv

A ghost-girl-rider. And though, toil-tried,
        He withers daily,
        Time touches her not,
        But she still rides gaily
        In his rapt thought

On that shagged and shaly
     Atlantic spot,
     And as when first eyed
Draws rein and sings to the swing of the tide.

1913

The Spell of the Rose*

'I mean to build a hall anon,
     And shape two turrets there,
     And a broad newelled stair,
And a cool well for crystal water;
     Yes; I will build a hall anon,
     Plant roses love shall feed upon,
     And apple-trees and pear.'

He set to build the manor-hall,
     And shaped the turrets there,
     And the broad newelled stair,
And the cool well for crystal water;
     He built for me that manor-hall,
     And planted many trees withal,
     But no rose anywhere.

And as he planted never a rose
     That bears the flower of love,
     Though other flowers throve
Some heart-bane moved our souls to sever
     Since he had planted never a rose;
     And misconceits raised horrid shows,
     And agonies came thereof.

'I'll mend these miseries,' then said I,
     And so, at dead of night,
     I went and, screened from sight,
That nought should keep our souls in severance,
     I set a rose-bush. 'This,' said I,
     'May end divisions dire and wry,
     And long-drawn days of blight.'

But I was called from earth – yea, called
    Before my rose-bush grew;
    And would that now I knew
What feels he of the tree I planted,
    And whether, after I was called
    To be a ghost, he, as of old,
        Gave me his heart anew!

Perhaps now blooms that queen of trees
    I set but saw not grow,
    And he, beside its glow –
Eyes couched of the mis-vision that blurred me –
    Ay, there beside that queen of trees
    He sees me as I was, though sees
        Too late to tell me so!

St Launce's Revisited*

    Slip back, Time!
    Yet again I am nearing
    Castle and keep, uprearing
        Gray, as in my prime.

    At the inn
    Smiling nigh, why is it
    Not as on my visit
        When hope and I were twin?

    Groom and jade
    Whom I found here, moulder;
    Strange the tavern-holder,
        Strange the tap-maid.

    Here I hired
    Horse and man for bearing
    Me on my wayfaring
        To the door desired.

Evening gloomed
As I journeyed forward
To the faces shoreward,
  Till their dwelling loomed.

If again
Towards the Atlantic sea there
I should speed, they'd be there
  Surely now as then? . . .

Why waste thought,
When I know them vanished
Under earth; yea, banished
  Ever into nought!

Where the Picnic Was

Where we made the fire
In the summer time
Of branch and briar
On the hill to the sea,
I slowly climb
Through winter mire,
And scan and trace
The forsaken place
Quite readily.

Now a cold wind blows,
And the grass is gray,
But the spot still shows
As a burnt circle – aye,
And stick-ends, charred,
Still strew the sward
Whereon I stand,
Last relic of the band
Who came that day!

Yes, I am here
Just as last year,
And the sea breathes brine

From its strange straight line
Up hither, the same
As when we four came.
— But two have wandered far
From this grassy rise
Into urban roar
Where no picnics are,
And one — has shut her eyes
For evermore.

from MISCELLANEOUS PIECES

Her Secret

That love's dull smart distressed my heart
 He shrewdly learnt to see,
But that I was in love with a dead man
 Never suspected he.

He searched for the trace of a pictured face,
 He watched each missive come,
And a sheet that seemed like a love-line
 Wrought his look lurid and numb.

He dogged my feet to the city street,
 He followed me to the sea,
But not to the nigh, still churchyard
 Did he dream of following me!

She Charged Me

She charged me with having said this and that
To another woman long years before,
In the very parlour where we sat, —

Sat on a night when the endless pour
Of rain on the roof and the road below
Bent the spring of the spirit more and more. . . .

– So charged she me; and the Cupid's bow
Of her mouth was hard, and her eyes, and her face,
And her white forefinger lifted slow.

Had she done it gently, or shown a trace
That not too curiously would she view
A folly flown ere her reign had place,

A kiss might have closed it. But I knew
From the fall of each word, and the pause between,
That the curtain would drop upon us two
Ere long, in our play of slave and queen.

The Newcomer's Wife

He paused on the sill of a door ajar
That screened a lively liquor-bar,
For the name had reached him through the door
Of her he had married the week before.

'We called her the Hack of the Parade;
But she was discreet in the games she played;
If slightly worn, she's pretty yet,
And gossips, after all, forget:

'And he knows nothing of her past;
I am glad the girl's in luck at last;
Such ones, though stale to native eyes,
Newcomers snatch at as a prize.'

'Yes, being a stranger he sees her blent
Of all that's fresh and innocent,
Nor dreams how many a love-campaign
She had enjoyed before his reign!'

That night there was the splash of a fall
Over the slimy harbour-wall:
They searched, and at the deepest place
Found him with crabs upon his face.

Had You Wept

Had you wept; had you but neared me with a hazed uncertain ray,
Dewy as the face of the dawn, in your large and luminous eye,
Then would have come back all the joys the tidings had slain that
    day,
And a new beginning, a fresh fair heaven, have smoothed the
    things awry.
But you were less feebly human, and no passionate need for clinging
Possessed your soul to overthrow reserve when I came near;
Ay, though you suffer as much as I from storms the hours are
    bringing
Upon your heart and mine, I never see you shed a tear.

The deep strong woman is weakest, the weak one is the strong;
The weapon of all weapons best for winning, you have not used;
Have you never been able, or would you not, through the evil
    times and long?
Has not the gift been given you, or such gift have you refused?
When I bade me not absolve you on that evening or the morrow,
Why did you not make war on me with those who weep like rain?
You felt too much, so gained no balm for all your torrid sorrow,
And hence our deep division, and our dark undying pain.

In the British Museum

'What do you see in that time-touched stone,
        When nothing is there
But ashen blankness, although you give it
        A rigid stare?

'You look not quite as if you saw,
        But as if you heard,
Parting your lips, and treading softly
        As mouse or bird.

'It is only the base of a pillar, they'll tell you,
    That came to us
From a far old hill men used to name
    Areopagus.'

— 'I know no art, and I only view
    A stone from a wall,
But I am thinking that stone has echoed
    The voice of Paul;

'Paul as he stood and preached beside it
    Facing the crowd,
A small gaunt figure with wasted features,
    Calling out loud

'Words that in all their intimate accents
    Pattered upon
That marble front, and were wide reflected,
    And then were gone.

'I'm a labouring man, and know but little,
    Or nothing at all;
But I can't help thinking that stone once echoed
    The voice of Paul.'

Seen by the Waits

Through snowy woods and shady
    We went to play a tune
To the lonely manor-lady
    By the light of the Christmas moon.

We violed till, upward glancing
    To where a mirror leaned,
It showed her airily dancing,
    Deeming her movements screened;

Dancing alone in the room there,
　　Thin-draped in her robe of night;
Her postures, glassed in the gloom there,
　　Were a strange phantasmal sight.

She had learnt (we heard when homing)
　　That her roving spouse was dead:
Why she had danced in the gloaming
　　We thought, but never said.

In the Days of Crinoline

A plain tilt-bonnet on her head
She took the path across the leaze.
– Her spouse the vicar, gardening, said,
'Too dowdy that, for coquetries,
　　　　So I can hoe at ease.'

But when she had passed into the heath,
And gained the wood beyond the flat,
She raised her skirts, and from beneath
Unpinned and drew as from a sheath
　　　　An ostrich-feathered hat.

And where the hat had hung she now
Concealed and pinned the dowdy hood,
And set the hat upon her brow,
And thus emerging from the wood
　　　　Tripped on in jaunty mood.

The sun was low and crimson-faced
As two came that way from the town,
And plunged into the wood untraced. . . .
When severally therefrom they paced
　　　　The sun had quite gone down.

The hat and feather disappeared,
The dowdy hood again was donned,
And in the gloom the fair one neared

Her home and husband dour, who conned
    Calmly his blue-eyed blonde.

'To-day,' he said, 'you have shown good sense,
A dress so modest and so meek
Should always deck your goings hence
Alone.' And as a recompense
    He kissed her on the cheek.

The Workbox

'See, here's the workbox, little wife,
    That I made of polished oak.'
He was a joiner, of village life;
    She came of borough folk.

He holds the present up to her
    As with a smile she nears
And answers to the profferer,
    ''Twill last all my sewing years!'

'I warrant it will. And longer too.
    'Tis a scantling that I got
Off poor John Wayward's coffin, who
    Died of they knew not what.

'The shingled pattern that seems to cease
    Against your box's rim
Continues right on in the piece
    That's underground with him.

'And while I worked it made me think
    Of timber's varied doom;
One inch where people eat and drink,
    The next inch in a tomb.

'But why do you look so white, my dear,
    And turn aside your face?
You knew not that good lad, I fear,
    Though he came from your native place?'

'How could I know that good young man,
    Though he came from my native town,
When he must have left far earlier than
    I was a woman grown?'

'Ah, no. I should have understood!
    It shocked you that I gave
To you one end of a piece of wood
    Whose other is in a grave?'

'Don't, dear, despise my intellect,
    Mere accidental things
Of that sort never have effect
    On my imaginings.'

Yet still her lips were limp and wan,
    Her face still held aside,
As if she had known not only John,
    But known of what he died.

The Satin Shoes

'If ever I walk to church to wed,
    As other maidens use,
And face the gathered eyes,' she said,
    'I'll go in satin shoes!'

She was as fair as early day
    Shining on meads unmown,
And her sweet syllables seemed to play
    Like flute-notes softly blown.

The time arrived when it was meet
    That she should be a bride;
The satin shoes were on her feet,
    Her father was at her side.

They stood within the dairy door,
　　And gazed across the green;
The church loomed on the distant moor,
　　But rain was thick between.

'The grass-path hardly can be stepped,
　　The lane is like a pool!' –
Her dream is shown to be inept,
　　Her wish they overrule.

'To go forth shod in satin soft
　　A coach would be required!'
For thickest boots the shoes were doffed –
　　Those shoes her soul desired. . . .

All day the bride, as overborne,
　　Was seen to brood apart,
And that the shoes had not been worn
　　Sat heavy on her heart.

From her wrecked dream, as months flew on,
　　Her thought seemed not to range.
'What ails the wife,' they said anon,
　　'That she should be so strange?'. . .

Ah – what coach comes with furtive glide –
　　A coach of closed-up kind?
It comes to fetch the last year's bride,
　　Who wanders in her mind.

She strove with them, and fearfully ran
　　Stairward with one low scream:
'Nay – coax her,' said the madhouse man,
　　'With some old household theme.'

'If you will go, dear, you must fain
　　Put on those shoes – the pair
Meant for your marriage, which the rain
　　Forbade you then to wear.'

She clapped her hands, flushed joyous hues;
    'O yes – I'll up and ride
If I am to wear my satin shoes
    And be a proper bride!'

Out then her little foot held she,
    As to depart with speed;
The madhouse man smiled pleasantly
    To see the wile succeed.

She turned to him when all was done,
    And gave him her thin hand,
Exclaiming like an enraptured one,
    'This time it will be grand!'

She mounted with a face elate,
    Shut was the carriage door;
They drove her to the madhouse gate,
    And she was seen no more. . . .

Yet she was fair as early day
    Shining on meads unmown,
And her sweet syllables seemed to play
    Like flute-notes softly blown.

Exeunt Omnes

i

Everybody else, then, going,
And I still left where the fair was? . . .
Much have I seen of neighbour loungers
    Making a lusty showing,
    Each now past all knowing.

ii

There is an air of blankness
In the street and the littered spaces;
Thoroughfare, steeple, bridge and highway
    Wizen themselves to lankness;
    Kennels dribble dankness.

iii
Folk all fade. And whither,
As I wait alone where the fair was?
Into the clammy and numbing night-fog
Whence they entered hither.
Soon one more goes thither!

*2 June 1913**

from SATIRES OF CIRCUMSTANCE
IN FIFTEEN GLIMPSES*

(*First published April 1911*)

xi. In the Restaurant

'But hear. If you stay, and the child be born,
It will pass as your husband's with the rest,
While, if we fly, the teeth of scorn
Will be gleaming at us from east to west;
And the child will come as a life despised;
I feel an elopement is ill-advised!'

'O you realize not what it is, my dear,
To a woman! Daily and hourly alarms
Lest the truth should out. How can I stay here
And nightly take him into my arms!
Come to the child no name or fame,
Let us go, and face it, and bear the shame.'

xii. At the Draper's

'I stood at the back of the shop, my dear,
But you did not perceive me.
Well, when they deliver what you were shown
I shall know nothing of it, believe me!'

And he coughed and coughed as she paled and said,
  'O, I didn't see you come in there –
Why couldn't you speak?' – 'Well, I didn't. I left
  That you should not notice I'd been there.

'You were viewing some lovely things. "*Soon required
  For a widow, of latest fashion*;"
And I knew 'twould upset you to meet the man
  Who had to be cold and ashen

'And screwed in a box before they could dress you
  "*In the last new note in mourning*,"
As they defined it. So, not to distress you,
  I left you to your adorning.'

from

MOMENTS OF VISION AND
MISCELLANEOUS VERSES

Moments of Vision

That mirror
Which makes of men a transparency,
   Who holds that mirror
And bids us such a breast-bare spectacle see
   Of you and me?

That mirror
Whose magic penetrates like a dart,
   Who lifts that mirror
And throws our mind back on us, and our heart,
   Until we start?

That mirror
Works well in these night hours of ache;
   Why in that mirror
Are tincts we never see ourselves once take
   When the world is awake?

That mirror
Can test each mortal when unaware;
   Yea, that strange mirror
May catch his last thoughts, whole life foul or fair,
   Glassing it – where?

We Sat at the Window*

(Bournemouth, 1875)

We sat at the window looking out,
And the rain came down like silken strings
That Swithin's day. Each gutter and spout
Babbled unchecked in the busy way
   Of witless things:
Nothing to read, nothing to see
Seemed in that room for her and me
   On Swithin's day.

We were irked by the scene, by our own selves; yes,
For I did not know, nor did she infer
How much there was to read and guess
By her in me, and to see and crown
   By me in her.
Wasted were two souls in their prime,
And great was the waste, that July time
   When the rain came down.

Afternoon Service at Mellstock

(Circa 1850)

On afternoons of drowsy calm
   We stood in the panelled pew,
Singing one-voiced a Tate-and-Brady psalm
   To the tune of 'Cambridge New'.

We watched the elms, we watched the rooks,
   The clouds upon the breeze,
Between the whiles of glancing at our books,
   And swaying like the trees.

So mindless were those outpourings! –
   Though I am not aware
That I have gained by subtle thought on things
   Since we stood psalming there.

At the Word 'Farewell'*

She looked like a bird from a cloud
   On the clammy lawn,
Moving alone, bare-browed
   In the dim of dawn.
The candles alight in the room
   For my parting meal
Made all things withoutdoors loom
   Strange, ghostly, unreal.

The hour itself was a ghost,
    And it seemed to me then
As of chances the chance furthermost
    I should see her again.
I beheld not where all was so fleet
    That a Plan of the past
Which had ruled us from birthtime to meet
    Was in working at last:

No prelude did I there perceive
    To a drama at all,
Or foreshadow what fortune might weave
    From beginnings so small;
But I rose as if quicked by a spur
    I was bound to obey,
And stepped through the casement to her
    Still alone in the gray.

'I am leaving you. . . . Farewell!' I said,
    As I followed her on
By an alley bare boughs overspread;
    'I soon must be gone!'
Even then the scale might have been turned
    Against love by a feather,
— But crimson one cheek of hers burned
    When we came in together.

First Sight of Her and After*

A day is drawing to its fall
    I had not dreamed to see;
The first of many to enthrall
    My spirit, will it be?
Or is this eve the end of all
    Such new delight for me?

I journey home: the pattern grows
    Of moonshades on the way:
'Soon the first quarter, I suppose,'
    Sky-glancing travellers say;
I realize that it, for those,
    Has been a common day.

*Near Lanivet, 1872**

There was a stunted handpost just on the crest,
    Only a few feet high:
She was tired, and we stopped in the twilight-time for her rest,
    At the crossways close thereby.

She leant back, being so weary, against its stem,
    And laid her arms on its own,
Each open palm stretched out to each end of them,
    Her sad face sideways thrown.

Her white-clothed form at this dim-lit cease of day
    Made her look as one crucified
In my gaze at her from the midst of the dusty way,
    And hurriedly 'Don't,' I cried.

I do not think she heard. Loosing thence she said,
    As she stepped forth ready to go,
'I am rested now. – Something strange came into my head;
    I wish I had not leant so!'

And wordless we moved onward down from the hill
    In the west cloud's murked obscure,
And looking back we could see the handpost still
    In the solitude of the moor.

'It struck her too,' I thought, for as if afraid
    She heavily breathed as we trailed;
Till she said, 'I did not think how 'twould look in the shade,
    When I leant there like one nailed.'

I, lightly: 'There's nothing in it. For *you*, anyhow!'
    – 'O I know there is not,' said she . . .
'Yet I wonder . . . If no one is bodily crucified now,
    In spirit one may be!'

And we dragged on and on, while we seemed to see
    In the running of Time's far glass
Her crucified, as she had wondered if she might be
    Some day. – Alas, alas!

Quid Hic Agis? *

i

When I weekly knew
An ancient pew,
And murmured there
The forms of prayer
And thanks and praise
In the ancient ways,
And heard read out
During August drought
That chapter from Kings
Harvest-time brings;
– How the prophet, broken
By griefs unspoken,
Went heavily away
To fast and to pray,
And, while waiting to die,
The Lord passed by,
And a whirlwind and fire
Drew nigher and nigher,
And a small voice anon
Bade him up and be gone, –
I did not apprehend
As I sat to the end
And watched for her smile
Across the sunned aisle,
That this tale of a seer
Which came once a year
Might, when sands were heaping,
Be like a sweat creeping,
Or in any degree
Bear on her or on me!

ii

When later, by chance
Of circumstance,
It befel me to read
On a hot afternoon
At the lectern there
The selfsame words
As the lesson decreed,
To the gathered few
From the hamlets near –
Folk of flocks and herds
Sitting half aswoon,
Who listened thereto
As women and men
Not overmuch
Concerned at such –
So, like them then,
I did not see
What drought might be
With me, with her,
As the Kalendar
Moved on, and Time
Devoured our prime.

iii

But now, at last,
When our glory has passed,
And there is no smile
From her in the aisle,
But where it once shone
A marble, men say,
With her name thereon
Is discerned to-day;
And spiritless
In the wilderness
I shrink from sight
And desire the night,
(Though, as in old wise,
I might still arise,
Go forth, and stand
And prophesy in the land),

I feel the shake
Of wind and earthquake,
And consuming fire
Nigher and nigher,
And the voice catch clear,
'What doest thou here?'

The Spectator: 1916. During the War

On a Midsummer Eve

I idly cut a parsley stalk,
And blew therein towards the moon;
I had not thought what ghosts would walk
With shivering footsteps to my tune.

I went, and knelt, and scooped my hand
As if to drink, into the brook,
And a faint figure seemed to stand
Above me, with the bygone look.

I lipped rough rhymes of chance, not choice,
I thought not what my words might be;
There came into my ear a voice
That turned a tenderer verse for me.

The Blinded Bird

So zestfully canst thou sing?
And all this indignity,
With God's consent, on thee!
Blinded ere yet a-wing
By the red-hot needle thou,
I stand and wonder how
So zestfully thou canst sing!

Resenting not such wrong,
Thy grievous pain forgot,
Eternal dark thy lot,
Groping thy whole life long,
After that stab of fire;
Enjailed in pitiless wire;
Resenting not such wrong!

Who hath charity? This bird.*
Who suffereth long and is kind,
Is not provoked, though blind
And alive ensepulchred?
Who hopeth, endureth all things?
Who thinketh no evil, but sings?
Who is divine? This bird.

I Travel as a Phantom Now

I travel as a phantom now,
For people do not wish to see
In flesh and blood so bare a bough
    As Nature makes of me.

And thus I visit bodiless
Strange gloomy households often at odds,
And wonder if Man's consciousness
    Was a mistake of God's.

And next I meet you, and I pause,
And think that if mistake it were,
As some have said, O then it was
    One that I well can bear!

1915

Lines

To a Movement in Mozart's E-Flat Symphony

Show me again the time
When in the Junetide's prime
We flew by meads and mountains northerly! –
Yea, to such freshness, fairness, fulness, fineness, freeness,
    Love lures life on.

Show me again the day
When from the sandy bay
We looked together upon the pestered sea! –
Yea, to such surging, swaying, sighing, swelling, shrinking,
    Love lures life on.

Show me again the hour
When by the pinnacled tower
We eyed each other and feared futurity! –
Yea, to such bodings, broodings, beatings, blanchings, blessings,
    Love lures life on.

Show me again just this:
The moment of that kiss
Away from the prancing folk, by the strawberry-tree! –
Yea, to such rashness, ratheness, rareness, ripeness, richness,
    Love lures life on.

Begun November 1898

His Heart

A Woman's Dream

At midnight, in the room where he lay dead
Whom in his life I had never clearly read,
I thought if I could peer into that citadel
His heart, I should at last know full and well

What hereto had been known to him alone,
Despite our long sit-out of years foreflown,
'And if,' I said, 'I do this for his memory's sake,
It would not wound him, even if he could wake.'

So I bent over him. He seemed to smile
With a calm confidence the whole long while
That I, withdrawing his heart, held it and, bit by bit,
Perused the unguessed things found written on it.

It was inscribed like a terrestrial sphere
With quaint vermiculations close and clear —
His graving. Had I known, would I have risked the stroke
Its reading brought, and my own heart nigh broke!

Yes, there at last, eyes opened, did I see
His whole sincere symmetric history;
There were his truth, his simple singlemindedness,
Strained, maybe, by time's storms, but there no less.

There were the daily deeds from sun to sun
In blindness, but good faith, that he had done;
There were regrets, at instances wherein he swerved
(As he conceived) from cherishings I had deserved.

There were old hours all figured down as bliss —
Those spent with me — (how little had I thought this!)
There those when, at my absence, whether he slept or waked,
(Though I knew not 'twas so!) his spirit ached.

There that when we were severed, how day dulled
Till time joined us anew, was chronicled:
And arguments and battlings in defence of me
That heart recorded clearly and ruddily.

I put it back, and left him as he lay
While pierced the morning pink and then the gray
Into each dreary room and corridor around,
Where I shall wait, but his step will not sound.

Something Tapped

Something tapped on the pane of my room
  When there was never a trace
Of wind or rain, and I saw in the gloom
  My weary Belovéd's face.

'O I am tired of waiting,' she said,
  'Night, morn, noon, afternoon;
So cold it is in my lonely bed,
  And I thought you would join me soon!'

I rose and neared the window-glass,
  But vanished thence had she:
Only a pallid moth, alas,
  Tapped at the pane for me.

August 1913

A Kiss

By a wall the stranger now calls his,
Was born of old a particular kiss,
Without forethought in its genesis;
Which in a trice took wing on the air.
And where that spot is nothing shows:
    There ivy calmly grows,
    And no one knows
    What a birth was there!

That kiss is gone where none can tell –
Not even those who felt its spell:
It cannot have died; that know we well.
Somewhere it pursues its flight,
One of a long procession of sounds
    Travelling aethereal rounds
    Far from earth's bounds
    In the infinite.

The Oxen*

Christmas Eve, and twelve of the clock.
   'Now they are all on their knees,'
An elder said as we sat in a flock
   By the embers in hearthside ease.

We pictured the meek mild creatures where
   They dwelt in their strawy pen,
Nor did it occur to one of us there
   To doubt they were kneeling then.

So fair a fancy few would weave
   In these years! Yet, I feel,
If someone said on Christmas Eve,
   'Come; see the oxen kneel

'In the lonely barton by yonder coomb
   Our childhood used to know,'
I should go with him in the gloom,
   Hoping it might be so.

1915

The Photograph

The flame crept up the portrait line by line
As it lay on the coals in the silence of night's profound,
   And over the arm's incline,
And along the marge of the silkwork superfine,
And gnawed at the delicate bosom's defenceless round.

Then I vented a cry of hurt, and averted my eyes;
The spectacle was one that I could not bear,
   To my deep and sad surprise;
But, compelled to heed, I again looked furtivewise
Till the flame had eaten her breasts, and mouth, and hair.

'Thank God, she is out of it now!' I said at last,
In a great relief of heart when the thing was done
   That had set my soul aghast,

And nothing was left of the picture unsheathed from the past
But the ashen ghost of the card it had figured on.

She was a woman long hid amid packs of years,
She might have been living or dead; she was lost to my sight,
    And the deed that had nigh drawn tears
Was done in a casual clearance of life's arrears;
But I felt as if I had put her to death that night! . . .
           ·   ·   ·

– Well; she knew nothing thereof did she survive,
And suffered nothing if numbered among the dead;
    Yet – yet – if on earth alive
Did she feel a smart, and with vague strange anguish strive?
If in heaven, did she smile at me sadly and shake her head?

Transformations

Portion of this yew
Is a man my grandsire knew,
Bosomed here at its foot:
This branch may be his wife,
A ruddy human life
Now turned to a green shoot.

These grasses must be made
Of her who often prayed,
Last century, for repose;
And the fair girl long ago
Whom I often tried to know
May be entering this rose.

So, they are not underground,
But as nerves and veins abound
In the growths of upper air,
And they feel the sun and rain,
And the energy again
That made them what they were!

The Last Signal

(11 October 1886)

A Memory of William Barnes

Silently I footed by an uphill road
That led from my abode to a spot yew-boughed;
Yellowly the sun sloped low down to westward,
    And dark was the east with cloud.

Then, amid the shadow of that livid sad east,
    Where the light was least, and a gate stood wide,
Something flashed the fire of the sun that was facing it,
    Like a brief blaze on that side.

Looking hard and harder I knew what it meant —
    The sudden shine sent from the livid east scene;
It meant the west mirrored by the coffin of my friend there,
    Turning to the road from his green,

To take his last journey forth — he who in his prime
    Trudged so many a time from that gate athwart the land!
Thus a farewell to me he signalled on his grave-way,
    As with a wave of his hand.

Winterborne-Came Path

The Figure in the Scene

It pleased her to step in front and sit
    Where the cragged slope was green,
While I stood back that I might pencil it
    With her amid the scene;
        Till it gloomed and rained;
But I kept on, despite the drifting wet
    That fell and stained
My draught, leaving for curious quizzings yet
    The blots engrained.

And thus I drew her there alone,
    Seated amid the gauze

Of moisture, hooded, only her outline shown,
    With rainfall marked across.
      – Soon passed our stay;
Yet her rainy form is the Genius still of the spot,
    Immutable, yea,
Though the place now knows her no more, and has known her not
    Ever since that day.

From an old note

Love the Monopolist

(*Young Lover's Reverie*)

The train draws forth from the station-yard,
    And with it carries me.
I rise, and stretch out, and regard
    The platform left, and see
An airy slim blue form there standing,
    And know that it is she.

While with strained vision I watch on,
    The figure turns round quite
To greet friends gaily; then is gone. . . .
    The import may be slight,
But why remained she not hard gazing
    Till I was out of sight?

'O do not chat with others there,'
    I brood. 'They are not I.
O strain your thoughts as if they were
    Gold bands between us; eye
All neighbour scenes as so much blankness
    Till I again am by!

'A troubled soughing in the breeze
    And the sky overhead
Let yourself feel; and shadeful trees,
    Ripe corn, and apples red,
Read as things barren and distasteful
    While we are separated!

'When I come back uncloak your gloom,
    And let in lovely day;
Then the long dark as of the tomb
    Can well be thrust away
With sweet things I shall have to practise,
    And you will have to say!'

Begun 1871: finished —

Overlooking the River Stour*

The swallows flew in the curves of an eight
    Above the river-gleam
    In the wet June's last beam:
Like little crossbows animate
The swallows flew in the curves of an eight
    Above the river-gleam.

Planing up shavings of crystal spray
    A moor-hen darted out
    From the bank thereabout,
And through the stream-shine ripped his way;
Planing up shavings of crystal spray
    A moor-hen darted out.

Closed were the kingcups; and the mead
    Dripped in monotonous green,
    Though the day's morning sheen
Had shown it golden and honeybee'd;
Closed were the kingcups; and the mead
    Dripped in monotonous green.

And never I turned my head, alack,
    While these things met my gaze
    Through the pane's drop-drenched glaze,
To see the more behind my back. . . .
O never I turned, but let, alack,
    These less things hold my gaze!

Old Furniture

I know not how it may be with others
    Who sit amid relics of householdry
That date from the days of their mothers' mothers,
    But well I know how it is with me
        Continually.

I see the hands of the generations
    That owned each shiny familiar thing
In play on its knobs and indentations,
    And with its ancient fashioning
        Still dallying:

Hands behind hands, growing paler and paler,
    As in a mirror a candle-flame
Shows images of itself, each frailer
    As it recedes, though the eye may frame
        Its shape the same.

On the clock's dull dial a foggy finger,
    Moving to set the minutes right
With tentative touches that lift and linger
    In the wont of a moth on a summer night,
        Creeps to my sight.

On this old viol, too, fingers are dancing –
    As whilom – just over the strings by the nut,
The tip of a bow receding, advancing
    In airy quivers, as if it would cut
        The plaintive gut.

And I see a face by that box for tinder,
    Glowing forth in fits from the dark,
And fading again, as the linten cinder
    Kindles to red at the flinty spark,
        Or goes out stark.

Well, well. It is best to be up and doing,
    The world has no use for one to-day

Who eyes things thus — no aim pursuing!
He should not continue in this stay,
But sink away.

The Interloper

'And I saw the figure and visage of Madness seeking for a home'

There are three folk driving in a quaint old chaise,
And the cliff-side track looks green and fair;
I view them talking in quiet glee
As they drop down towards the puffins' lair
By the roughest of ways;
But another with the three rides on, I see,
Whom I like not to be there!

No: it's not anybody you think of. Next
A dwelling appears by a slow sweet stream
Where two sit happy and half in the dark:
They read, helped out by a frail-wick'd gleam,
Some rhythmic text;
But one sits with them whom they don't mark,
One I'm wishing could not be there.

No: not whom you knew and name. And now
I discern gay diners in a mansion-place,
And the guests dropping wit — pert, prim, or choice,
And the hostess's tender and laughing face,
And the host's bland brow;
But I cannot help hearing a hollow voice,
And I'd fain not hear it there.

No: it's not from the stranger you met once. Ah,
Yet a goodlier scene than that succeeds;
People on a lawn — quite a crowd of them. Yes,
And they chatter and ramble as fancy leads;
And they say, 'Hurrah!'
To a blithe speech made; save one, mirthless,
Who ought not to be there.

Nay: it's not the pale Form your imagings raise,
That waits on us all at a destined time,
It is not the Fourth Figure the Furnace showed;*
O that it were such a shape sublime
          In these latter days!
It is that under which best lives corrode;
          Would, would it could not be there!

Logs on the Hearth

A Memory of a Sister*

The fire advances along the log
          Of the tree we felled,
Which bloomed and bore striped apples by the peck
     Till its last hour of bearing knelled.

The fork that first my hand would reach
          And then my foot
In climbings upward inch by inch, lies now
     Sawn, sapless, darkening with soot..

Where the bark chars is where, one year,
          It was pruned, and bled –
Then overgrew the wound. But now, at last,
     Its growings all have stagnated.

My fellow-climber rises dim
          From her chilly grave –
Just as she was, her foot near mine on the bending limb,
     Laughing, her young brown hand awave.

December 1915

The Sunshade

Ah – it's the skeleton of a lady's sunshade,
     Here at my feet in the hard rock's chink,
     Merely a naked sheaf of wires! –
     Twenty years have gone with their livers and diers
     Since it was silked in its white or pink.

Noonshine riddles the ribs of the sunshade,
  No more a screen from the weakest ray;
  Nothing to tell us the hue of its dyes,
  Nothing but rusty bones as it lies
  In its coffin of stone, unseen till to-day.

Where is the woman who carried that sunshade
  Up and down this seaside place? —
  Little thumb standing against its stem,
  Thoughts perhaps bent on a love-stratagem,
  Softening yet more the already soft face!

Is the fair woman who carried that sunshade
  A skeleton just as her property is,
  Laid in the chink that none may scan?
  And does she regret — if regret dust can —
  The vain things thought when she flourished this?

Swanage Cliffs

The Wind's Prophecy

I travel on by barren farms,
And gulls glint out like silver flecks
Against a cloud that speaks of wrecks,
And bellies down with black alarms.
I say: 'Thus from my lady's arms
I go; those arms I love the best!'
The wind replies from dip and rise,
'Nay; toward her arms thou journeyest.'

A distant verge morosely gray
Appears, while clots of flying foam
Break from its muddy monochrome,
And a light blinks up far away.
I sigh: 'My eyes now as all day
Behold her ebon loops of hair!'
Like bursting bonds the wind responds,
'Nay, wait for tresses flashing fair!'

From tides the lofty coastlands screen
Come smitings like the slam of doors,
Or hammerings on hollow floors,
As the swell cleaves through caves unseen.
Say I: 'Though broad this wild terrene,
Her city home is matched of none!'
From the hoarse skies the wind replies:
'Thou shouldst have said her sea-bord one.'

The all-prevailing clouds exclude
The one quick timorous transient star;
The waves outside where breakers are
Huzza like a mad multitude.
'Where the sun ups it, mist-imbued,'
I cry, 'there reigns the star for me!'
The wind outshrieks from points and peaks:
'Here, westward, where it downs, mean ye!'

Yonder the headland, vulturine,
Snores like old Skrymer in his sleep,
And every chasm and every steep
Blackens as wakes each pharos-shine.
'I roam, but one is safely mine,'
I say. 'God grant she stay my own!'
Low laughs the wind as if it grinned:
'Thy Love is one thou'st not yet known.'

Rewritten from an old copy

During Wind and Rain

They sing their dearest songs –
He, she, all of them – yea,
Treble and tenor and bass,
    And one to play;
With the candles mooning each face. . . .
    Ah, no; the years O!
How the sick leaves reel down in throngs!

They clear the creeping moss —
Elders and juniors — aye,
Making the pathways neat
    And the garden gay;
And they build a shady seat. . . .
    Ah, no; the years, the years;
See, the white storm-birds wing across!

They are blithely breakfasting all —
Men and maidens — yea,
Under the summer tree,
    With a glimpse of the bay,
While pet fowl come to the knee. . . .
    Ah, no; the years O!
And the rotten rose is ript from the wall.

They change to a high new house,
He, she, all of them — aye,
Clocks and carpets and chairs
    On the lawn all day,
And brightest things that are theirs. . . .
    Ah, no; the years, the years;
Down their carved names the rain-drop ploughs.

A Backward Spring

The trees are afraid to put forth buds,
And there is timidity in the grass;
The plots lie gray where gouged by spuds,
    And whether next week will pass
Free of sly sour winds is the fret of each bush
    Of barberry waiting to bloom.

Yet the snowdrop's face betrays no gloom,
And the primrose pants in its heedless push,
Though the myrtle asks if it's worth the fight
    This year with frost and rime
    To venture one more time
On delicate leaves and buttons of white
From the selfsame bough as at last year's prime,

And never to ruminate on or remember
What happened to it in mid-December.

April 1917

Who's in the Next Room?

'Who's in the next room? – who?
    I seemed to see
Somebody in the dawning passing through,
    Unknown to me.'
'Nay: you saw nought. He passed invisibly.'

'Who's in the next room? – who?
    I seem to hear
Somebody muttering firm in a language new
    That chills the ear.'
'No: you catch not his tongue who has entered there.'

'Who's in the next room? – who?
    I seem to feel
His breath like a clammy draught, as if it drew
    From the Polar Wheel.'
'No: none who breathes at all does the door conceal.'

'Who's in the next room? – who?
    A figure wan
With a message to one in there of something due?
    Shall I know him anon?'
'Yea he; and he brought such; and you'll know him anon.

*I Thought, My Heart**

I thought, my Heart, that you had healed
Of those sore smartings of the past,
And that the summers had oversealed
    All mark of them at last.
But closely scanning in the night
I saw them standing crimson-bright

Just as she made them:
Nothing could fade them;
Yea, I can swear
That there they were —
They still were there!

Then the Vision of her who cut them came,
And looking over my shoulder said,
'I am sure you deal me all the blame
     For those sharp smarts and red;
But meet me, dearest, to-morrow night,
In the churchyard at the moon's half-height,
     And so strange a kiss
     Shall be mine, I wis,
     That you'll cease to know
     If the wounds you show
     Be there or no!'

*Midnight on the Great Western**

In the third-class seat sat the journeying boy,
     And the roof-lamp's oily flame
Played down on his listless form and face,
Bewrapt past knowing to what he was going,
     Or whence he came.

In the band of his hat the journeying boy
     Had a ticket stuck; and a string
Around his neck bore the key of his box,
That twinkled gleams of the lamp's sad beams
     Like a living thing.

What past can be yours, O journeying boy
     Towards a world unknown,
Who calmly, as if incurious quite
On all at stake, can undertake
     This plunge alone?

Knows your soul a sphere, O journeying boy,
     Our rude realms far above,

Whence with spacious vision you mark and mete
This region of sin that you find you in,
     But are not of?

*The Clock-Winder**

It is dark as a cave,
Or a vault in the nave
When the iron door
Is closed, and the floor
Of the church relaid
With trowel and spade.

But the parish-clerk
Cares not for the dark
As he winds in the tower
At a regular hour
The rheumatic clock
Whose dilatory knock
You can hear when praying
At the day's decaying,
Or at any lone while
From a pew in the aisle.

Up, up from the ground
Around and around
In the turret stair
He clambers, to where
The wheelwork is,
With its tick, click, whizz,
Reposefully measuring
Each day to its end
That mortal men spend
In sorrowing and pleasuring.
Nightly thus does he climb
To the trackway of Time.

Him I followed one night
To this place without light,
And, ere I spoke, heard

Him say, word by word,
At the end of his winding,
The darkness unminding: —

'So I wipe out one more,
My Dear, of the sore
Sad days that still be,
Like a drying Dead Sea,
Between you and me!'

Who she was no man knew:
He had long borne him blind
To all womankind;
And was ever one who
Kept his past out of view.

The Shadow on the Stone

I went by the Druid stone
That broods in the garden white and lone,
And I stopped and looked at the shifting shadows
That at some moments fall thereon
From the tree hard by with a rhythmic swing,
And they shaped in my imagining
To the shade that a well-known head and shoulders
Threw there when she was gardening.

I thought her behind my back,
Yea, her I long had learned to lack,
And I said: 'I am sure you are standing behind me,
Though how do you get into this old track?'
And there was no sound but the fall of a leaf
As a sad response; and to keep down grief
I would not turn my head to discover
That there was nothing in my belief.

Yet I wanted to look and see
That nobody stood at the back of me;

But I thought once more: 'Nay, I'll not unvision
  A shape which, somehow, there may be.'
So I went on softly from the glade,
  And left her behind me throwing her shade,
As she were indeed an apparition —
  My head unturned lest my dream should fade.

Begun 1913: finished 1916

The Choirmaster's Burial*

He often would ask us
That, when he died,
After playing so many
To their last rest,
If out of us any
Should here abide,
And it would not task us,
We would with our lutes
Play over him
By his grave-brim
The psalm he liked best —
The one whose sense suits
'Mount Ephraim' —
And perhaps we should seem
To him, in Death's dream,
Like the seraphim.

As soon as I knew
That his spirit was gone
I thought this his due,
And spoke thereupon.

'I think,' said the vicar,
'A read service quicker
Than viols out-of-doors
In these frosts and hoars.
That old-fashioned way
Requires a fine day,

And it seems to me
It had better not be.'

Hence, that afternoon,
Though never knew he
That his wish could not be,
To get through it faster
They buried the master
Without any tune.

But 'twas said that, when
At the dead of next night
The vicar looked out,
There struck on his ken
Thronged roundabout,
Where the frost was graying
The headstoned grass,
A band all in white
Like the saints in church-glass,
Singing and playing
The ancient stave
By the choirmaster's grave.

Such the tenor man told
When he had grown old.

While Drawing in a Churchyard

'It is sad that so many of worth,
    Still in the flesh,' soughed the yew,
'Misjudge their lot whom kindly earth
    Secludes from view.

'They ride their diurnal round
    Each day-span's sum of hours
In peerless ease, without jolt or bound
    Or ache like ours.

'If the living could but hear
What is heard by my roots as they creep
Round the restful flock, and the things said there,
No one would weep.'

' "Now set among the wise,"
They say: "Enlarged in scope,
That no God trumpet us to rise
We truly hope." '

I listened to his strange tale
In the mood that stillness brings,
And I grew to accept as the day wore pale
That show of things.

from POEMS OF WAR AND PATRIOTISM

Men Who March Away*

(Song of the Soldiers)

What of the faith and fire within us
Men who march away
Ere the barn-cocks say
Night is growing gray,
Leaving all that here can win us;
What of the faith and fire within us
Men who march away?

Is it a purblind prank, O think you,
Friend with the musing eye,
Who watch us stepping by
With doubt and dolorous sigh?
Can much pondering so hoodwink you!
Is it a purblind prank, O think you,
Friend with the musing eye?

Nay. We well see what we are doing,
  Though some may not see —
  Dalliers as they be —
  England's need are we;
Her distress would leave us rueing:
Nay. We well see what we are doing,
  Though some may not see!

In our heart of hearts believing
  Victory crowns the just,
  And that braggarts must
  Surely bite the dust,
Press we to the field ungrieving,
In our heart of hearts believing
  Victory crowns the just.

Hence the faith and fire within us
  Men who march away
  Ere the barn-cocks say
  Night is growing gray,
Leaving all that here can win us;
Hence the faith and fire within us
  Men who march away.

5 September 1914

In Time of 'The Breaking of Nations'

i
Only a man harrowing clods
  In a slow silent walk
With an old horse that stumbles and nods
  Half asleep as they stalk.

ii
Only thin smoke without flame
  From the heaps of couch-grass;
Yet this will go onward the same
  Though Dynasties pass.

iii

Yonder a maid and her wight
 Come whispering by:
War's annals will cloud into night
 Ere their story die.

1915

NOTE – (Title) Jer., LI 20*

from FINALE

The Coming of the End

How it came to an end!
The meeting afar from the crowd,
And the love-looks and laughters unpenned,
The parting when much was avowed,
 How it came to an end!

It came to an end;
Yes, the outgazing over the stream,
With the sun on each serpentine bend,
Or, later, the luring moon-gleam;
 It came to an end.

It came to an end,
The housebuilding, furnishing, planting,
As if there were ages to spend
In welcoming, feasting, and jaunting;
 It came to an end.

It came to an end,
That journey of one day a week:
('It always goes on,' said a friend,
'Just the same in bright weathers or bleak;')
 But it came to an end.

'*How* will come to an end
This orbit so smoothly begun,
Unless some convulsion attend?'
I often said. 'What will be done
  When it comes to an end?'

Well, it came to an end
Quite silently — stopped without jerk;
Better close no prevision could lend;
Working out as One planned it should work
  Ere it came to an end.

Afterwards

When the Present has latched its postern behind my tremulous
    stay,
  And the May month flaps its glad green leaves like wings,
Delicate-filmed as new-spun silk, will the neighbours say,
  'He was a man who used to notice such things'?

If it be in the dusk when, like an eyelid's soundless blink,
  The dewfall-hawk comes crossing the shades to alight
Upon the wind-warped upland thorn, a gazer may think,
  'To him this must have been a familiar sight.'

If I pass during some nocturnal blackness, mothy and warm,
  When the hedgehog travels furtively over the lawn,
One may say, 'He strove that such innocent creatures should come
    to no harm,
  But he could do little for them; and now he is gone.'

If, when hearing that I have been stilled at last, they stand at the
    door,
  Watching the full-starred heavens that winter sees,
Will this thought rise on those who will meet my face no more,
  'He was one who had an eye for such mysteries'?

And will any say when my bell of quittance is heard in the gloom,
  And a crossing breeze cuts a pause in its outrollings,
Till they rise again, as they were a new bell's boom,
  'He hears it not now, but used to notice such things'?

from
LATE LYRICS AND EARLIER

Weathers

i

This is the weather the cuckoo likes,
    And so do I;
When showers betumble the chestnut spikes,
    And nestlings fly:
And the little brown nightingale bills his best,
And they sit outside at 'The Travellers' Rest',
And maids come forth sprig-muslin drest,
And citizens dream of the south and west,
    And so do I.

ii

This is the weather the shepherd shuns,
    And so do I;
When beeches drip in browns and duns,
    And thresh, and ply;
And hill-hid tides throb, throe on throe,
And meadow rivulets overflow,
And drops on gate-bars hang in a row,
And rooks in families homeward go,
    And so do I.

Faintheart in a Railway Train*

At nine in the morning there passed a church,
At ten there passed me by the sea,
At twelve a town of smoke and smirch,
At two a forest of oak and birch,
    And then, on a platform, she:

A radiant stranger, who saw not me.
I said, 'Get out to her do I dare?'
But I kept my seat in my search for a plea,
And the wheels moved on. O could it but be
    That I had alighted there!

The Garden Seat

Its former green is blue and thin,
And its once firm legs sink in and in;
Soon it will break down unaware,
Soon it will break down unaware.

At night when reddest flowers are black
Those who once sat thereon come back;
Quite a row of them sitting there,
Quite a row of them sitting there.

With them the seat does not break down,
Nor winter freeze them, nor floods drown,
For they are as light as upper air,
They are as light as upper air!

A Man Was Drawing Near to Me*

On that gray night of mournful drone,
Apart from aught to hear, to see,
I dreamt not that from shires unknown
     In gloom, alone,
     By Halworthy,
A man was drawing near to me.

I'd no concern at anything,
No sense of coming pull-heart play;
Yet, under the silent outspreading
     Of even's wing
     Where Otterham lay,
A man was riding up my way.

I thought of nobody — not of one,
But only of trifles — legends, ghosts —
Though, on the moorland dim and dun
     That travellers shun
     About these coasts,
The man had passed Tresparret Posts.

There was no light at all inland,
Only the seaward pharos-fire,
Nothing to let me understand
    That hard at hand
    By Hennett Byre
The man was getting nigh and nigher.

There was a rumble at the door,
A draught disturbed the drapery,
And but a minute passed before,
    With gaze that bore
    My destiny,
The man revealed himself to me.

The Contretemps

A forward rush by the lamp in the gloom,
    And we clasped, and almost kissed;
But she was not the woman whom
I had promised to meet in the thawing brume
On that harbour-bridge; nor was I he of her tryst.

So loosening from me swift she said:
    'O why, why feign to be
The one I had meant! – to whom I have sped
To fly with, being so sorrily wed!'
– 'Twas thus and thus that she upbraided me.

My assignation had struck upon
    Some others' like it, I found.
And her lover rose on the night anon;
And then her husband entered on
The lamplit, snowflaked, sloppiness around.

'Take her and welcome, man!' he cried:
    'I wash my hands of her.
I'll find me twice as good a bride!'
    – All this to me, whom he had eyed,
Plainly, as his wife's planned deliverer.

And next the lover: 'Little I knew,
    Madam, you had a third!
Kissing here in my very view!'
    — Husband and lover then withdrew.
I let them; and I told them not they erred.

Why not? Well, there faced she and I —
    Two strangers, who'd kissed, or near,
Chancewise. To see stand weeping by
    A woman once embraced, will try
The tension of a man the most austere.

So it began; and I was young,
    She pretty, by the lamp,
As flakes came waltzing down among
    The waves of her clinging hair, that hung
Heavily on her temples, dark and damp.

And there alone still stood we two;
    She one cast off for me,
Or so it seemed: while night ondrew,
    Forcing a parley what should do
We twain hearts caught in one catastrophe.

In stranded souls a common strait
    Wakes latencies unknown,
Whose impulse may precipitate
    A life-long leap. The hour was late,
And there was the Jersey boat with its funnel agroan.

'Is wary walking worth much pother?'
    It grunted, as still it stayed.
'One pairing is as good as another
    Where all is venture! Take each other,
And scrap the oaths that you have aforetime made.' . . .

    — Of the four involved there walks but one
        On earth at this late day.
    And what of the chapter so begun?

In that odd complex what was done?
Well; happiness comes in full to none:
Let peace lie on lulled lips: I will not say.

Weymouth

A Night in November

I marked when the weather changed,
And the panes began to quake,
And the winds rose up and ranged,
That night, lying half-awake.

Dead leaves blew into my room,
And alighted upon my bed,
And a tree declared to the gloom
Its sorrow that they were shed.

One leaf of them touched my hand,
And I thought that it was you
There stood as you used to stand,
And saying at last you knew!

(?) *1913*

The Fallow Deer at the Lonely House*

One without looks in to-night
    Through the curtain-chink
From the sheet of glistening white;
One without looks in to-night
    As we sit and think
    By the fender-brink.

We do not discern those eyes
    Watching in the snow;
Lit by lamps of rosy dyes
We do not discern those eyes
    Wondering, aglow,
    Fourfooted, tiptoe.

The Selfsame Song

A bird sings the selfsame song,
With never a fault in its flow,
That we listened to here those long
    Long years ago.

A pleasing marvel is how
A strain of such rapturous rote
Should have gone on thus till now
    Unchanged in a note!

— But it's not the selfsame bird. —
No: perished to dust is he. . . .
As also are those who heard
    That song with me.

At the Railway Station, Upway

'There is not much that I can do,
  For I've no money that's quite my own!'
  Spoke up the pitying child —
A little boy with a violin
At the station before the train came in, —
'But I can play my fiddle to you,
And a nice one 'tis, and good in tone!'

  The man in the handcuffs smiled;
The constable looked, and he smiled, too,
  As the fiddle began to twang;
And the man in the handcuffs suddenly sang
    With grimful glee:
    'This life so free
    Is the thing for me!'
And the constable smiled, and said no word,
As if unconscious of what he heard;
And so they went on till the train came in —
The convict, and boy with the violin.

An Autumn Rain-Scene

There trudges one to a merry-making
    With a sturdy swing,
    On whom the rain comes down.

To fetch the saving medicament
    Is another bent,
    On whom the rain comes down.

One slowly drives his herd to the stall
    Ere ill befall,
    On whom the rain comes down.

This bears his missives of life and death
    With quickening breath,
    On whom the rain comes down.

One watches for signals of wreck or war
    From the hill afar,
    On whom the rain comes down.

No care if he gain a shelter or none,
    Unhired moves one,
    On whom the rain comes down.

On the Tune Called the Old-Hundred-and-Fourth *

We never sang together
    Ravenscroft's terse old tune
On Sundays or on weekdays,
In sharp or summer weather,
    At night-time or at noon.

Why did we never sing it,
    Why never so incline
On Sundays or on weekdays,

Even when soft wafts would wing it
  From your far floor to mine?

Shall we that tune, then, never
  Stand voicing side by side
On Sundays or on weekdays? . . .
Or shall we, when for ever
  In Sheol we abide,

Sing it in desolation,
  As we might long have done
On Sundays or on weekdays
With love and exultation
  Before our sands had run?

Voices from Things Growing in a Churchyard*

These flowers are I, poor Fanny Hurd,
    Sir or Madam,
A little girl here sepultured.
Once I flit-fluttered like a bird
Above the grass, as now I wave
In daisy shapes above my grave,
    All day cheerily,
    All night eerily!

— I am one Bachelor Bowring, 'Gent',
    Sir or Madam;
In shingled oak my bones were pent;
Hence more than a hundred years I spent
In my feat of change from a coffin-thrall
To a dancer in green as leaves on a wall,
    All day cheerily,
    All night eerily!

— I, these berries of juice and gloss,
    Sir or Madam,
Am clean forgotten as Thomas Voss;

Thin-urned, I have burrowed away from the moss
That covers my sod, and have entered this yew,
And turned to clusters ruddy of view,
    All day cheerily,
    All night eerily!

– The Lady Gertrude, proud, high-bred,
        Sir or Madam,
Am I – this laurel that shades your head;
Into its veins I have stilly sped,
And made them of me; and my leaves now shine,
As did my satins superfine,
    All day cheerily,
    All night eerily!

– I, who as innocent withwind climb,
        Sir or Madam,
Am one Eve Greensleeves, in olden time
Kissed by men from many a clime,
Beneath sun, stars, in blaze, in breeze,
As now by glowworms and by bees,
    All day cheerily,
    All night eerily!

– I'm old Squire Audeley Grey, who grew,
        Sir or Madam,
Aweary of life, and in scorn withdrew;
Till anon I clambered up anew
As ivy-green, when my ache was stayed,
And in that attire I have longtime gayed
    All day cheerily,
    All night eerily!

– And so these maskers breathe to each
        Sir or Madam
Who lingers there, and their lively speech
Affords an interpreter much to teach,
As their murmurous accents seem to come

Thence hitheraround in a radiant hum,
          All day cheerily,
          All night eerily!

NOTE – (Stanza 5) It was said her real name was Eve Trevillian or Trevelyan; and that she
was the handsome mother of two or three illegitimate children, *circa* 1784–95.

A Two-Years' Idyll*

          Yes; such it was;
        Just those two seasons unsought,
    Sweeping like summertide wind on our ways;
          Moving, as straws,
        Hearts quick as ours in those days;
    Going like wind, too, and rated as nought
          Save as the prelude to plays
          Soon to come – larger, life-fraught:
          Yes; such it was.

          'Nought' it was called,
        Even by ourselves – that which springs
    Out of the years for all flesh, first or last,
          Commonplace, scrawled
          Dully on days that go past.
    Yet, all the while, it upbore us like wings
          Even in hours overcast:
          Aye, though this best thing of things,
          'Nought' it was called!

          What seems it now?
        Lost: such beginning was all;
    Nothing came after: romance straight forsook
          Quickly somehow
          Life when we sped from our nook,
    Primed for new scenes with designs smart and tall. . . .
          – A preface without any book,
          A trumpet uplipped, but no call;
          That seems it now.

If You Had Known

If you had known
When listening with her to the far-down moan
Of the white-selvaged and empurpled sea,
And rain came on that did not hinder talk,
Or damp your flashing facile gaiety
In turning home, despite the slow wet walk
By crooked ways, and over stiles of stone;
    If you had known

    You would lay roses,
Fifty years thence, on her monument, that discloses
Its graying shape upon the luxuriant green;
Fifty years thence to an hour, by chance led there,
What might have moved you? — yea, had you foreseen
That on the tomb of the selfsame one, gone where
The dawn of every day is as the close is,
    You would lay roses!

1920

I Look in Her Face

(*Song: Minor*)

I look in her face and say,
'Sing as you used to sing
About Love's blossoming;'
But she hints not Yea or Nay.

'Sing, then, that Love's a pain,
If, Dear, you think it so,
Whether it be or no;'
But dumb her lips remain.

I go to a far-off room,
A faint song ghosts my ear;
Which song I cannot hear,
But it seems to come from a tomb.

They Would Not Come

I travelled to where in her lifetime
　She'd knelt at morning prayer,
　To call her up as if there;
But she paid no heed to my suing,
As though her old haunt could win not
　A thought from her spirit, or care.

I went where my friend had lectioned
　The prophets in high declaim,
　That my soul's ear the same
Full tones should catch as aforetime;
But silenced by gear of the Present
　Was the voice that once there came!

Where the ocean had sprayed our banquet
　I stood, to recall it as then:
　The same eluding again!
No vision. Shows contingent
Affrighted it further from me
　Even than from my home-den.

When I found them no responders,
　But fugitives prone to flee
　From where they had used to be,
It vouched I had been led hither
As by night wisps in bogland,
　And bruised the heart of me!

After a Romantic Day

The railway bore him through
An earthen cutting out from a city:
　There was no scope for view,
Though the frail light shed by a slim young moon
　Fell like a friendly tune.

Fell like a liquid ditty,
And the blank lack of any charm
    Of landscape did no harm.
The bald steep cutting, rigid, rough,
    And moon-lit, was enough
For poetry of place: its weathered face
Formed a convenient sheet whereon
The visions of his mind were drawn.

A Procession of Dead Days

I see the ghost of a perished day;
I know his face, and the feel of his dawn:
'Twas he who took me far away
    To a spot strange and gray:
Look at me, Day, and then pass on,
But come again: yes, come anon!

Enters another into view;
His features are not cold or white,
But rosy as a vein seen through:
    Too soon he smiles adieu.
Adieu, O ghost-day of delight;
But come and grace my dying sight.

Enters the day that brought the kiss:
He brought it in his foggy hand
To where the mumbling river is,
    And the high clematis;
It lent new colour to the land,
And all the boy within me manned.

Ah, this one. Yes, I know his name,
He is the day that wrought a shine
Even on a precinct common and tame,
    As 'twere of purposed aim.
He shows him as a rainbow sign
Of promise made to me and mine.

The next stands forth in his morning clothes,
And yet, despite their misty blue,
They mark no sombre custom-growths
   That joyous living loathes,
But a meteor act, that left in its queue
A train of sparks my lifetime through.

I almost tremble at his nod —
This next in train — who looks at me
As I were slave, and he were god
   Wielding an iron rod.
I close my eyes; yet still is he
In front there, looking mastery.

In semblance of a face averse
The phantom of the next one comes:
I did not know what better or worse
   Chancings might bless or curse
When his original glossed the thrums
Of ivy, bringing that which numbs.

Yes; trees were turning in their sleep
Upon their windy pillows of gray
When he stole in. Silent his creep
   On the grassed eastern steep. . . .
I shall not soon forget that day,
And what his third hour took away!

Outside the Casement

(A Reminiscence of the War)

We sat in the room
And praised her whom
We saw in the portico-shade outside:
   She could not hear
   What was said of her,
But smiled, for its purport we did not hide.

   Then in was brought
   That message, fraught

With evil fortune for her out there,
　　Whom we loved that day
　　More than any could say,
And would fain have fenced from a waft of care.

　　And the question pressed
　　Like lead on each breast,
Should we cloak the tidings, or call her and tell?
　　It was too intense
　　A choice for our sense,
As we pondered and watched her we loved so well.

　　Yea, spirit failed us
　　At what assailed us;
How long, while seeing what soon must come,
　　Should we counterfeit
　　No knowledge of it,
And stay the stroke that would blanch and numb?

　　And thus, before
　　For evermore
Joy left her, we practised to beguile
　　Her innocence when
　　She now and again
Looked in, and smiled us another smile.

On a Discovered Curl of Hair

When your soft welcomings were said,
This curl was waving on your head,
And when we walked where breakers dinned
It sported in the sun and wind,
And when I had won your words of grace
It brushed and clung about my face.
Then, to abate the misery
Of absentness, you gave it me.

Where are its fellows now? Ah, they
For brightest brown have donned a gray,
And gone into a caverned ark,
Ever unopened, always dark!

Yet this one curl, untouched of time,
Beams with live brown as in its prime,
So that it seems I even could now
Restore it to the living brow
By bearing down the western road
Till I had reached your old abode.

February 1913

Just the Same

I sat. It all was past;
Hope never would hail again;
Fair days had ceased at a blast,
The world was a darkened den.

The beauty and dream were gone,
And the halo in which I had hied
So gaily gallantly on
Had suffered blot and died!

I went forth, heedless whither,
In a cloud too black for name:
— People frisked hither and thither;
The world was just the same.

The Sun's Last Look on the Country Girl

(M.H.)

The sun threw down a radiant spot
   On the face in the winding-sheet —
The face it had lit when a babe's in its cot;
And the sun knew not, and the face knew not
   That soon they would no more meet.

Now that the grave has shut its door,
   And lets not in one ray,

Do they wonder that they meet no more –
That face and its beaming visitor –
    That met so many a day?

December 1915

Epitaph

I never cared for Life: Life cared for me,
And hence I owed it some fidelity.
It now says, 'Cease; at length thou hast learnt to grind
Sufficient toll for an unwilling mind,
And I dismiss thee – not without regard
That thou didst ask no ill-advised reward,
Nor sought in me much more than thou couldst find.'

An Ancient to Ancients

Where once we danced, where once we sang,
    Gentlemen,
The floors are sunken, cobwebs hang,
And cracks creep; worms have fed upon
The doors. Yea, sprightlier times were then
Than now, with harps and tabrets gone,
    Gentlemen!

Where once we rowed, where once we sailed,
    Gentlemen,
And damsels took the tiller, veiled
Against too strong a stare (God wot
Their fancy, then or anywhen!)
Upon that shore we are clean forgot,
    Gentlemen!

We have lost somewhat, afar and near,
    Gentlemen,
The thinning of our ranks each year
Affords a hint we are nigh undone,
That we shall not be ever again

The marked of many, loved of one,
      Gentlemen.

In dance the polka hit our wish,
      Gentlemen,
The paced quadrille, the spry schottische,
'Sir Roger'. – And in opera spheres
The 'Girl' (the famed 'Bohemian'),
And 'Trovatore', held the ears,
      Gentlemen.

This season's paintings do not please,
      Gentlemen,
Like Etty, Mulready, Maclise;
Throbbing romance has waned and wanned;
No wizard wields the witching pen
Of Bulwer, Scott, Dumas, and Sand,
      Gentlemen.

The bower we shrined to Tennyson,
      Gentlemen,
Is roof-wrecked; damps there drip upon
Sagged seats, the creeper-nails are rust,
The spider is sole denizen;
Even she who voiced those rhymes is dust,
      Gentlemen!

We who met sunrise sanguine-souled,
      Gentlemen,
Are wearing weary. We are old;
These younger press; we feel our rout
Is imminent to Aïdes' den, –
That evening shades are stretching out,
      Gentlemen!

And yet, though ours be failing frames,
      Gentlemen,
So were some others' history names,
Who trode their track light-limbed and fast
As these youth, and not alien

From enterprise, to their long last,
    Gentlemen.

Sophocles, Plato, Socrates,
    Gentlemen,
Pythagoras, Thucydides,
Herodotus, and Homer, – yea,
Clement, Augustin, Origen,
Burnt brightlier towards their setting-day,
    Gentlemen.

And ye, red-lipped and smooth-browed; list,
    Gentlemen;
Much is there waits you we have missed;
Much lore we leave you worth the knowing,
Much, much has lain outside our ken:
Nay, rush not: time serves: we are going,
    Gentlemen.

Surview

'Cogitavi vias meas'*

A cry from the green-grained sticks of the fire
    Made me gaze where it seemed to be:
'Twas my own voice talking therefrom to me
On how I had walked when my sun was higher –
    My heart in its arrogancy.

'*You held not to whatsoever was true,*'
    Said my own voice talking to me:
'*Whatsoever was just you were slack to see;*
Kept not things lovely and pure in view,'
    Said my own voice talking to me.

'*You slighted her that endureth all,*'
    Said my own voice talking to me;
'*Vaunteth not, trusteth hopefully;*
That suffereth long and is kind withal,'
    Said my own voice talking to me.

'*You taught not that which you set about,*'
    Said my own voice talking to me;
'*That the greatest of things is Charity. . . .*'
– And the sticks burnt low, and the fire went out,
    And my voice ceased talking to me.

from

HUMAN SHOWS, FAR PHANTASIES, SONGS, AND TRIFLES

Waiting Both

A star looks down at me,
And says: 'Here I and you
Stand, each in our degree:
What do you mean to do, –
    Mean to do?'

I say: 'For all I know,
Wait, and let Time go by,
Till my change come.'* – 'Just so,'
The star says: 'So mean I: –
    So mean I.'

A Bird-Scene at a Rural Dwelling

When the inmate stirs, the birds retire discreetly
From the window-ledge, whereon they whistled sweetly
    And on the step of the door,
    In the misty morning hoar;
  But now the dweller is up they flee
  To the crooked neighbouring codlin-tree;
And when he comes fully forth they seek the garden,
And call from the lofty costard, as pleading pardon
    For shouting so near before
    In their joy at being alive: –
Meanwhile the hammering clock within goes five.

I know a domicile of brown and green,
Where for a hundred summers there have been
Just such enactments, just such daybreaks seen.

The Later Autumn

Gone are the lovers, under the bush
    Stretched at their ease;
    Gone the bees,

Tangling themselves in your hair as they rush
    On the line of your track,
    Leg-laden, back
    With a dip to their hive
    In a prepossessed dive.

Toadsmeat is mangy, frosted, and sere;
    Apples in grass
    Crunch as we pass,
And rot ere the men who make cyder appear.
    Couch-fires abound
    On fallows around,
    And shades far extend
    Like lives soon to end.

Spinning leaves join the remains shrunk and brown
    Of last year's display
    That lie wasting away,
On whose corpses they earlier as scorners gazed down
    From their aery green height:
    Now in the same plight
    They huddle; while yon
    A robin looks on.

Green Slates

(Penpethy)*

It happened once, before the duller
    Loomings of life defined them,
I searched for slates of greenish colour
    A quarry where men mined them;

And saw, the while I peered around there,
    In the quarry standing
A form against the slate background there,
    Of fairness eye-commanding.

And now, though fifty years have flown me,
    With all their dreams and duties,
And strange-pipped dice my hand has thrown me,
    And dust are all her beauties,

Green slates – seen high on roofs, or lower
    In waggon, truck, or lorry –
Cry out: 'Our home was where you saw her
    Standing in the quarry!'

At Rushy-Pond*

On the frigid face of the heath-hemmed pond
    There shaped the half-grown moon:
Winged whiffs from the north with a husky croon
    Blew over and beyond.

And the wind flapped the moon in its float on the pool,
    And stretched it to oval form;
Then corkscrewed it like a wriggling worm;
    Then wanned it weariful.

And I cared not for conning the sky above
    Where hung the substant thing,
For my thought was earthward sojourning
    On the scene I had vision of.

Since there it was once, in a secret year,
    I had called a woman to me
From across this water, ardently –
    And practised to keep her near;

Till the last weak love-words had been said,
    And ended was her time,
And blurred the bloomage of her prime,
    And white the earlier red.

And the troubled orb in the pond's sad shine
    Was her very wraith, as scanned
When she withdrew thence, mirrored, and
    Her days dropped out of mine.

When Dead

To——

It will be much better when
I am under the bough;
I shall be more myself, Dear, then,
Than I am now.

No sign of querulousness
To wear you out
Shall I show there: strivings and stress
Be quite without.

This fleeting life-brief blight
Will have gone past
When I resume my old and right
Place in the Vast.

And when you come to me
To show you true,
Doubt not I shall infallibly
Be waiting you.

Life and Death at Sunrise

(*Near Dogbury Gate, 1867*)

The hills uncap their tops
Of woodland, pasture, copse,
And look on the layers of mist
At their foot that still persist:
They are like awakened sleepers on one elbow lifted,
Who gaze around to learn if things during night have shifted.

A waggon creaks up from the fog
With a laboured leisurely jog;
Then a horseman from off the hill-tip
Comes clapping down into the dip;
While woodlarks, finches, sparrows, try to entune at one time,
And cocks and hens and cows and bulls take up the chime.

With a shouldered basket and flagon
A man meets the one with the waggon,
And both the men halt of long use.
'Well,' the waggoner says, 'what's the news?'
' – 'Tis a boy this time. You've just met the doctor trotting back.
She's doing very well. And we think we shall call him "Jack".

'And what have you got covered there?'
He nods to the waggon and mare.
'Oh, a coffin for old John Thinn:
We are just going to put him in.'
' – So he's gone at last. He always had a good constitution.'
' – He was ninety-odd. He could call up the French Revolution.'

Snow in the Suburbs*

Every branch big with it,
Bent every twig with it;
Every fork like a white web-foot;
Every street and pavement mute:
Some flakes have lost their way, and grope back upward, when
Meeting those meandering down they turn and descend again.
The palings are glued together like a wall,
And there is no waft of wind with the fleecy fall.

A sparrow enters the tree,
Whereon immediately
A snow-lump thrice his own slight size
Descends on him and showers his head and eyes,
And overturns him,
And near inurns him,
And lights on a nether twig, when its brush
Starts off a volley of other lodging lumps with a rush.

The steps are a blanched slope,
Up which, with feeble hope,
A black cat comes, wide-eyed and thin;
And we take him in.

The Frozen Greenhouse*

(St Juliot)

'There was a frost
Last night!' she said,
'And the stove was forgot
When we went to bed,
And the greenhouse plants
Are frozen dead!'

By the breakfast blaze
Blank-faced spoke she,
Her scared young look
Seeming to be
The very symbol
Of tragedy.

The frost is fiercer
Than then to-day,
As I pass the place
Of her once dismay,
But the greenhouse stands
Warm, tight, and gay,

While she who grieved
At the sad lot
Of her pretty plants –
Cold, iced, forgot –
Herself is colder,
And knows it not.

Two Lips

I kissed them in fancy as I came
Away in the morning glow:
I kissed them through the glass of her picture-frame:
She did not know.

I kissed them in love, in troth, in laughter,
    When she knew all; long so!
That I should kiss them in a shroud thereafter
    She did not know.

No Buyers

A Street Scene

A load of brushes and baskets and cradles and chairs
    Labours along the street in the rain:
With it a man, a woman, a pony with whiteybrown hairs. —
    The man foots in front of the horse with a shambling sway
        At a slower tread than a funeral train,
    While to a dirge-like tune he chants his wares,
Swinging a Turk's-head brush (in a drum-major's way
        When the bandsmen march and play).

A yard from the back of the man is the whiteybrown pony's nose:
He mirrors his master in every item of pace and pose:
        He stops when the man stops, without being told,
    And seems to be eased by a pause; too plainly he's old,
            Indeed, not strength enough shows
            To steer the disjointed waggon straight,
        Which wriggles left and right in a rambling line,
        Deflected thus by its own warp and weight,
        And pushing the pony with it in each incline.

            The woman walks on the pavement verge,
                Parallel to the man:
        She wears an apron white and wide in span,
    And carries a like Turk's-head, but more in nursing-wise:
            Now and then she joins in his dirge,
            But as if her thoughts were on distant things.
            The rain clams her apron till it clings. —
        So, step by step, they move with their merchandize,
                And nobody buys.

Last Love-Word*
(Song)

This is the last; the very, very last!
 Anon, and all is dead and dumb,
 Only a pale shroud over the past,
  That cannot be
  Of value small or vast,
  Love, then to me!

I can say no more: I have even said too much.
 I did not mean that this should come:
 I did not know 'twould swell to such —
  Nor, perhaps, you —
  When that first look and touch,
  Love, doomed us two!

189—

Nobody Comes*

Tree-leaves labour up and down,
 And through them the fainting light
 Succumbs to the crawl of night.
Outside in the road the telegraph wire
 To the town from the darkening land
Intones to travellers like a spectral lyre
 Swept by a spectral hand.

A car comes up, with lamps full-glare,
 That flash upon a tree:
 It has nothing to do with me,
And whangs along in a world of its own,
 Leaving a blacker air;
And mute by the gate I stand again alone,
 And nobody pulls up there.

9 October 1924

Last Look round St Martin's Fair

The sun is like an open furnace door,
Whose round revealed retort confines the roar
        Of fires beyond terrene;
The moon presents the lustre-lacking face
        Of a brass dial gone green,
        Whose hours no eye can trace.
The unsold heathcroppers are driven home
To the shades of the Great Forest whence they come
By men with long cord-waistcoats in brown monochrome.
The stars break out, and flicker in the breeze,
        It seems, that twitches the trees. –
        From its hot idol soon
The fickle unresting earth has turned to a fresh patroon –
        The cold, now brighter, moon.
The woman in red, at the nut-stall with the gun,
        Lights up, and still goes on:
She's redder in the flare-lamp than the sun
        Showed it ere it was gone.
Her hands are black with loading all the day,
And yet she treats her labour as 'twere play,
Tosses her ear-rings, and talks ribaldry
To the young men around as natural gaiety,
        And not a weary work she'd readily stay,
        And never again nut-shooting see,
        Though crying, 'Fire away!'

The Prospect

The twigs of the birch imprint the December sky
    Like branching veins upon a thin old hand;
I think of summer-time, yes, of last July,
    When she was beneath them, greeting a gathered band
        Of the urban and bland.

Iced airs wheeze through the skeletoned hedge from the north,
    With steady snores, and a numbing that threatens snow,

And skaters pass; and merry boys go forth
  To look for slides. But well, well do I know
    Whither I would go!

December 1912

When Oats Were Reaped

That day when oats were reaped, and wheat was ripe, and barley
    ripening,
  The road-dust hot, and the bleaching grasses dry,
    I walked along and said,
While looking just ahead to where some silent people lie:

'I wounded one who's there, and now know well I wounded her;
  But, ah, she does not know that she wounded me!'
    And not an air stirred,
Nor a bill of any bird; and no response accorded she.

August 1913

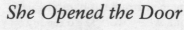

She Opened the Door

She opened the door of the West to me,
    With its loud sea-lashings,
    And cliff-side clashings
Of waters rife with revelry.

She opened the door of Romance to me,
    The door from a cell
    I had known too well,
Too long, till then, and was fain to flee.

She opened the door of a Love to me,
    That passed the wry
    World-welters by
As far as the arching blue the lea.

She opens the door of the Past to me,
    Its magic lights,
    Its heavenly heights,
When forward little is to see!

1913

The Harbour Bridge

From here, the quay, one looks above to mark
The bridge across the harbour, hanging dark
Against the day's-end sky, fair-green in glow
Over and under the middle archway's bow:
It draws its skeleton where the sun has set,
Yea, clear from cutwater to parapet;
On which mild glow, too, lines of rope and spar
    Trace themselves black as char.

Down here in shade we hear the painters shift
Against the bollards with a drowsy lift,
As moved by the incoming stealthy tide.
High up across the bridge the burghers glide
As cut black-paper portraits hastening on
In conversation none knows what upon:
Their sharp-edged lips move quickly word by word
    To speech that is not heard.

There trails the dreamful girl, who leans and stops,
There presses the practical woman to the shops,
There is a sailor, meeting his wife with a start,
And we, drawn nearer, judge they are keeping apart.
Both pause. She says: 'I've looked for you. I thought
We'd make it up.' Then no words can be caught.
At last: 'Won't you come home?' She moves still nigher:
    ''Tis comfortable, with a fire.'

'No,' he says gloomily. 'And, anyhow,
I can't give up the other woman now:
You should have talked like that in former days,
When I was last home.' They go different ways.

And the west dims, and yellow lamplights shine:
And soon above, like lamps more opaline,
White stars ghost forth, that care not for men's wives,
    Or any other lives.

Weymouth

At a Pause in a Country Dance

(*Middle of Last Century*)

They stood at the foot of the figure,
And panted: they'd danced it down through –
That 'Dashing White Serjeant' they loved so: –
A window, uncurtained, was nigh them
That end of the room. Thence in view

Outside it a valley updrew,
Where the frozen moon lit frozen snow:
At the furthermost reach of the valley
A light from a window shone low.
'They are inside that window,' said she,

As she looked. 'They sit up there for me;
And baby is sleeping there, too.'
He glanced. 'Yes,' he said. 'Never mind,
Let's foot our way up again; do!
And dance down the line as before.

'What's the world to us, meeting once more!'
' – Not much, when your husband full trusts you,
And thinks the child his that I bore!'
He was silent. The fiddlers six-eighted
With even more passionate vigour.

The pair swept again up the figure,
The child's cuckoo-father and she,
And the next couples threaded below,
And the twain wove their way to the top
Of 'The Dashing White Serjeant' they loved so,
Restarting: right, left, to and fro.

— From the homestead, seen yon, the small glow
Still adventured forth over the white,
Where the child slept, unknowing who sired it,
In the cradle of wicker tucked tight,
And its grandparents, nodding, admired it
In elbow-chairs through the slow night.

On the Portrait of a Woman about to be Hanged*

Comely and capable one of our race,
Posing there in your gown of grace,
Plain, yet becoming;
Could subtlest breast
Ever have guessed
What was behind that innocent face,
Drumming, drumming!

Would that your Causer, ere knoll your knell
For this riot of passion, might deign to tell
Why, since It made you
Sound in the germ,
It sent a worm
To madden Its handiwork, when It might well
Not have assayed you,

Not have implanted, to your deep rue,
The Clytaemnestra spirit in you,
And with purblind vision
Sowed a tare
In a field so fair,
And a thing of symmetry, seemly to view,
Brought to derision!

6 January 1923

Once at Swanage*

The spray sprang up across the cusps of the moon,
      And all its light loomed green
      As a witch-flame's weirdsome sheen
At the minute of an incantation scene;
And it greened our gaze — that night at demilune.

Roaring high and roaring low was the sea
      Behind the headland shores:
      It symboled the slamming of doors,
Or a regiment hurrying over hollow floors. . . .
And there we two stood, hands clasped; I and she!

Under High-Stoy Hill*

Four climbed High-Stoy from Ivelwards,
Where hedge meets hedge, and cart-ruts wind,
      Chattering like birds,
And knowing not what lay behind.

We laughed beneath the moonlight blink,
Said supper would be to our mind,
      And did not think
Of Time, and what might lie behind. . . .

The moon still meets that tree-tipped height,
The road — as then — still trails inclined;
      But since that night
We have well learnt what lay behind!

For all of the four then climbing here
But one are ghosts, and he brow-lined;
      With him they fare,
Yet speak not of what lies behind.

At the Mill

O Miller Knox, whom we knew well,
　　And the mill, and the floury floors,
And the corn, – and those two women,
　　　And infants – yours!

The sun was shining when you rode
　　To market on that day:
The sun was set when home-along
　　You ambled in the gray,
And gathered what had taken place
　　　While you were away.

O Miller Knox, 'twas grief to see
　　Your good wife hanging there
By her own rash and passionate hand,
　　　In a throe of despair;

And those two children, one by her,
　　And one by the waiting-maid,
Borne the same hour, and you afar,
　　　And she past aid.

And though sometimes you walk of nights,
　　Sleepless, to Yalbury Brow,
And glance the graveyard way, and grunt,
　　'Twas not much, anyhow:
She shouldn't ha' minded!' nought it helps
　　　To say that now.

And the water dribbles down your wheel,
　　Your mead blooms green and gold,
And birds 'twit in your apple-boughs
　　　Just as of old.

Retty's Phases*

i

Retty used to shake her head,
  Look with wicked eye;
Say, 'I'd tease you, simple Ned,
  If I cared to try!'
Then she'd hot-up scarlet red,
  Stilly step away,
Much afraid that what she'd said
  Sounded bold to say.

ii

Retty used to think she loved
  (Just a little) me.
Not untruly, as it proved
  Afterwards to be.
For, when weakness forced her rest
  If we walked a mile,
She would whisper she was blest
  By my clasp awhile.

iii

Retty used at last to say
  When she neared the Vale,
'Mind that you, Dear, on that day
  Ring my wedding peal!'
And we all, with pulsing pride,
  Vigorous sounding gave
Those six bells, the while outside
  John filled in her grave.

iv

Retty used to draw me down
  To the turfy heaps,
Where, with yeoman, squire, and clown
  Noticeless she sleeps.
Now her silent slumber-place
  Seldom do I know,

For when last I saw her face
　　Was so long ago!

From an old draft of 1868

NOTE – In many villages it was customary after the funeral of an unmarried young woman
to ring a peal as for her wedding while the grave was being filled in, as if Death were not to
be allowed to balk her of bridal honours. Young unmarried men were always her bearers.

A Popular Personage at Home

'I live here: "Wessex" is my name:
I am a dog known rather well:
I guard the house; but how that came
To be my whim I cannot tell.

'With a leap and a heart elate I go
At the end of an hour's expectancy
To take a walk of a mile or so
With the folk I let live here with me.

'Along the path, amid the grass
I sniff, and find out rarest smells
For rolling over as I pass
The open fields towards the dells.

'No doubt I shall always cross this sill,
And turn the corner, and stand steady,
Gazing back for my mistress till
She reaches where I have run already,

'And that this meadow with its brook,
And bulrush, even as it appears
As I plunge by with hasty look,
Will stay the same a thousand years.'

Thus 'Wessex'. But a dubious ray
At times informs his steadfast eye,
Just for a trice, as though to say,
'Yet, will this pass, and pass shall I?'

1924

Her Haunting-Ground

Can it be so? It must be so,
That visions have not ceased to be
In this the chiefest sanctuary
Of her whose form we used to know.
– Nay, but her dust is far away,
And 'where her dust is, shapes her shade,
If spirit clings to flesh,' they say:
Yet here her life-parts most were played!

Her voice explored this atmosphere,
Her foot impressed this turf around,
Her shadow swept this slope and mound,
Her fingers fondled blossoms here;
And so, I ask, why, why should she
Haunt elsewhere, by a slighted tomb,
When here she flourished sorrow-free,
And, save for others, knew no gloom?

A Parting-Scene

The two pale women cried,
But the man seemed to suffer more,
Which he strove hard to hide.
They stayed in the waiting-room, behind the door,
Till startled by the entering engine-roar,
As if they could not bear to have unfurled
Their misery to the eyes of all the world.

A soldier and his young wife
Were the couple; his mother the third,
Who had seen the seams of life.
He was sailing for the East I later heard.
– They kissed long, but they did not speak a word;
Then, strained, he went. To the elder the wife in tears
'Too long; too long!' burst out. ('Twas for five years.)

Shortening Days at the Homestead

The first fire since the summer is lit, and is smoking into the room:
   The sun-rays thread it through, like woof-lines in a loom.
   Sparrows spurt from the hedge, whom misgivings appal
That winter did not leave last year for ever, after all.
   Like shock-headed urchins, spiny-haired,
   Stand pollard willows, their twigs just bared.

Who is this coming with pondering pace,
Black and ruddy, with white embossed,
His eyes being black, and ruddy his face,
And the marge of his hair like morning frost?
     It's the cider-maker,
     And appletree-shaker,
And behind him on wheels, in readiness,
His mill, and tubs, and vat, and press.

That Moment

    The tragedy of that moment
      Was deeper than the sea,
    When I came in that moment
      And heard you speak to me!

    What I could not help seeing
      Covered life as a blot;
    Yes, that which I was seeing,
      And knew that you were not!

This Summer and Last

    Unhappy summer you,
      Who do not see
   What your yester-summer saw!
  Never, never will you be
      Its match to me,
    Never, never draw
   Smiles your forerunner drew,
      Know what it knew!

Divine things done and said
    Illumined it,
Whose rays crept into corn-brown curls,
Whose breezes heard a humorous wit
    Of fancy flit. –
  Still the alert brook purls,
  Though feet that there would tread
    Elsewhere have sped.

So, bran-new summer, you
    Will never see
All that yester-summer saw!
Never, never will you be
    In memory
  Its rival, never draw
  Smiles your forerunner drew,
    Know what it knew!

1913?

A Leaving

  Knowing what it bore
I watched the rain-smitten back of the car –
(Brown-curtained, such as the old ones were) –
When it started forth for a journey afar
Into the sullen November air,
And passed the glistening laurels and round the bend.

I have seen many gayer vehicles turn that bend
  In autumn, winter, and summer air,
  Bearing for journeys near or afar
  Many who now are not, but were,
  But I don't forget that rain-smitten car,
    Knowing what it bore!

Song to an Old Burden

The feet have left the wormholed flooring,
    That danced to the ancient air,
    The fiddler, all-ignoring,
Sleeps by the gray-grassed 'cello player:
Shall I then foot around around around,
    As once I footed there!

The voice is heard in the room no longer
    That trilled, none sweetlier,
    To gentle stops or stronger,
Where now the dust-draped cobwebs stir:
Shall I then sing again again again,
    As once I sang with her!

The eyes that beamed out rapid brightness
    Have longtime found their close,
    The cheeks have wanned to whiteness
That used to sort with summer rose:
Shall I then joy anew anew anew,
    As once I joyed in those!

O what's to me this tedious Maying,
    What's to me this June?
    O why should viols be playing
To catch and reel and rigadoon?
Shall I sing, dance around around around,
    When phantoms call the tune!

from

WINTER WORDS IN VARIOUS
MOODS AND METRES

Proud Songsters

The thrushes sing as the sun is going,
And the finches whistle in ones and pairs,
And as it gets dark loud nightingales
      In bushes
Pipe, as they can when April wears,
    As if all Time were theirs.

These are brand-new birds of twelve-months' growing,
Which a year ago, or less than twain,
No finches were, nor nightingales,
      Nor thrushes,
But only particles of grain,
    And earth, and air, and rain.

I Am the One

I am the one whom ringdoves see
      Through chinks in boughs
      When they do not rouse
      In sudden dread,
But stay on cooing, as if they said:
      'Oh; it's only he.'

I am the passer when up-eared hares,
      Stirred as they eat
      The new-sprung wheat,
      Their munch resume
As if they thought: 'He is one for whom
      Nobody cares.'

Wet-eyed mourners glance at me
      As in train they pass
      Along the grass
      To a hollowed spot,
And think: 'No matter; he quizzes not
      Our misery.'

I hear above: 'We stars must lend
             No fierce regard
             To his gaze, so hard
             Bent on us thus, –
Must scathe him not. He is one with us
             Beginning and end.'

To Louisa in the Lane*

Meet me again as at that time
    In the hollow of the lane;
I will not pass as in my prime
    I passed at each day's wane.
        – Ah, I remember!
To do it you will have to see
Anew this sorry scene wherein you have ceased to be!

But I will welcome your aspen form
    As you gaze wondering round
And say with spectral frail alarm,
    'Why am I still here found?
        – Ah, I remember!
It is through him with blitheful brow
Who did not love me then, but loves and draws me now!'

And I shall answer: 'Sweet of eyes,
    Carry me with you, Dear,
To where you donned this spirit-guise;
    It's better there than here!'
        – Till I remember
Such is a deed you cannot do:
Wait must I, till with flung-off flesh I follow you.

The Mound

For a moment pause: –
Just here it was;
And through the thin thorn hedge, by the rays of the moon,
I can see the tree in the field, and beside it the mound –

Now sheeted with snow — whereon we sat that June
    When it was green and round,
And she crazed my mind by what she coolly told —
    The history of her undoing,
(As I saw it), but she called 'comradeship',
    That bred in her no rueing:
    And saying she'd not be bound
For life to one man, young, ripe-yeared, or old,
Left me — an innocent simpleton to her viewing;
For, though my accompt of years outscored her own,
    Hers had more hotly flown. . . .
We never met again by this green mound,
To press as once so often lip on lip,
      And palter, and pause: —
      Yes; here it was!

The Lodging-House Fuchsias

    Mrs Masters's fuchsias hung
    Higher and broader, and brightly swung,
      Bell-like, more and more
    Over the narrow garden-path,
    Giving the passer a sprinkle-bath
      In the morning.

    She put up with their pushful ways,
    And made us tenderly lift their sprays,
      Going to her door:
    But when her funeral had to pass
    They cut back all the flowery mass
      In the morning.

Throwing a Tree

New Forest

The two executioners stalk along over the knolls,
Bearing two axes with heavy heads shining and wide,
And a long limp two-handled saw toothed for cutting great
    boles,
And so they approach the proud tree that bears the death-mark on
    its side.

Jackets doffed they swing axes and chop away just above
    ground,
And the chips fly about and lie white on the moss and fallen
    leaves;
Till a broad deep gash in the bark is hewn all the way round,
And one of them tries to hook upward a rope, which at last he
    achieves.

The saw then begins, till the top of the tall giant shivers:
The shivers are seen to grow greater each cut than before:
They edge out the saw, tug the rope; but the tree only quivers,
And kneeling and sawing again, they step back to try pulling once
    more.

Then, lastly, the living mast sways, further sways: with a
    shout
Job and Ike rush aside. Reached the end of its long staying
    powers
The tree crashes downward: it shakes all its neighbours
    throughout,
And two hundred years' steady growth has been ended in less than
    two hours.

Lying Awake

You, Morningtide Star, now are steady-eyed, over the east,
    I know it as if I saw you;
You, Beeches, engrave on the sky your thin twigs, even the least;
    Had I paper and pencil I'd draw you.

You, Meadow, are white with your counterpane cover of dew,
    I see it as if I were there;
You, Churchyard, are lightening faint from the shade of the yew,
    The names creeping out everywhere.

I Watched a Blackbird*

I watched a blackbird on a budding sycamore
One Easter Day, when sap was stirring twigs to the core;
    I saw his tongue, and crocus-coloured bill
    Parting and closing as he turned his trill;
    Then he flew down, seized on a stem of hay,
And upped to where his building scheme was under way,
As if so sure a nest were never shaped on spray.

A Nightmare, and the Next Thing

On this decline of Christmas Day
The empty street is fogged and blurred:
The house-fronts all seem backwise turned
As if the outer world were spurned:
Voices and songs within are heard,
Whence red rays gleam when fires are stirred,
Upon this nightmare Christmas Day.

The lamps, just lit, begin to outloom
Like dandelion-globes in the gloom;
The stonework, shop-signs, doors, look bald;
Curious crude details seem installed,
And show themselves in their degrees
As they were personalities
Never discerned when the street was bustling
With vehicles, and farmers hustling.

Three clammy casuals wend their way
To the Union House. I hear one say:
'Jimmy, this is a treat! Hay-hay!'

Six laughing mouths, six rows of teeth,
Six radiant pairs of eyes, beneath
Six yellow hats, looking out at the back
Of a waggonette on its slowed-down track
Up the steep street to some gay dance,
Suddenly interrupt my glance.

They do not see a gray nightmare
Astride the day, or anywhere.

The Felled Elm and She

When you put on that inmost ring
She, like you, was a little thing:
When your circles reached their fourth,
Scarce she knew life's south from north:
When your year-zones counted twenty
She had fond admirers plenty:
When you'd grown your twenty-second
She and I were lovers reckoned:
When you numbered twenty-three
She went everywhere with me:
When you, at your fortieth line,
Showed decay, she seemed to pine:
When you were quite hollow within
She was felled – mere bone and skin:
You too, lacking strength to grow
Further trunk-rings, were laid low,
Matching her; both unaware
That your lives formed such a pair.

After the Burial

The family had buried him,
　　　Their bread-bringer, their best:
They had returned to the house, whose hush a dim
　　　Vague vacancy expressed.

There sat his sons, mute, rigid-faced,
    His daughters, strained, red-eyed,
His wife, whose wan, worn features, vigil-traced,
    Bent over him when he died.

At once a peal bursts from the bells
    Of a large tall tower hard by:
Along the street the jocund clangour swells,
    And upward to the sky.

Probably it was a wedding-peal,
    Or possibly for a birth,
Or townsman knighted for political zeal,
    This resonant mark of mirth.

The mourners, heavy-browed, sat on
    Motionless. Well they heard,
They could not help it; nevertheless thereon
    Spoke not a single word,

Nor window did they close, to numb
    The bells' insistent calls
Of joy; but suffered the harassing din to come
    And penetrate their souls.

The Mongrel

In Havenpool Harbour the ebb was strong,
And a man with a dog drew near and hung,
And taxpaying day was coming along,
    So the mongrel had to be drowned.
The man threw a stick from the paved wharf-side
Into the midst of the ebbing tide,
And the dog jumped after with ardent pride
    To bring the stick aground.

But no: the steady suck of the flood
To seaward needed, to be withstood,
More than the strength of mongrelhood
    To fight its treacherous trend.

So, swimming for life with desperate will,
The struggler with all his natant skill
Kept buoyant in front of his master, still
    There standing to wait the end.

The loving eyes of the dog inclined
To the man he held as a god enshrined,
With no suspicion in his mind
    That this had all been meant.
Till the effort not to drift from shore
Of his little legs grew slower and slower,
And, the tide still outing with brookless power,
    Outward the dog, too, went.

Just ere his sinking what does one see
Break on the face of that devotee?
A wakening to the treachery
    He had loved with love so blind?
The faith that had shone in that mongrel's eye
That his owner would save him by and by
Turned to much like a curse as he sank to die,
    And a loathing of mankind.

We Field-Women

    How it rained
When we worked at Flintcomb-Ash,
And could not stand upon the hill
Trimming swedes for the slicing-mill.
The wet washed through us – plash, plash, plash:
    How it rained!

    How it snowed
When we crossed from Flintcomb-Ash
To the Great Barn for drawing reed,
Since we could nowise chop a swede. –
Flakes in each doorway and casement-sash:
    How it snowed!

How it shone
When we went from Flintcomb-Ash
To start at dairywork once more
In the laughing meads, with cows three-score,
And pails, and songs, and love — too rash:
How it shone!

'A Gentleman's Second-Hand Suit'

Here it is hanging in the sun
By the pawn-shop door,
A dress-suit — all its revels done
Of heretofore.
Long drilled to the waltzers' swing and sway,
As its tokens show:
What it has seen, what it could say
If it did but know!

The sleeve bears still a print of powder
Rubbed from her arms
When she warmed up as the notes swelled louder
And livened her charms —
Or rather theirs, for beauties many
Leant there, no doubt,
Leaving these tell-tale traces when he
Spun them about.

Its cut seems rather in bygone style
On looking close,
So it mayn't have bent it for some while
To the dancing pose:
Anyhow, often within its clasp
Fair partners hung,
Assenting to the wearer's grasp
With soft sweet tongue.

Where is, alas, the gentleman
Who wore this suit?
And where are his ladies? Tell none can:
Gossip is mute.

Some of them may forget him quite
Who smudged his sleeve,
Some think of a wild and whirling night
With him, and grieve.

We Say We Shall Not Meet

We say we shall not meet
Again beneath this sky,
And turn with leaden feet,
Murmuring 'Good-bye!'

But laugh at how we rued
Our former time's adieu
When those who went for good
Are met anew.

We talk in lightest vein
On trifles talked before,
And part to meet again,
But meet no more.

He Never Expected Much

[or]

A Consideration

[A reflection] on My Eighty-Sixth Birthday

Well, World, you have kept faith with me,
Kept faith with me;
Upon the whole you have proved to be
Much as you said you were.
Since as a child I used to lie
Upon the leaze and watch the sky,
Never, I own, expected I
That life would all be fair.

'Twas then you said, and since have said,
Times since have said,

In that mysterious voice you shed
    From clouds and hills around:
'Many have loved me desperately,
Many with smooth serenity,
While some have shown contempt of me
    Till they dropped underground.

'I do not promise overmuch,
    Child; overmuch;
Just neutral-tinted haps and such,'
    You said to minds like mine.
Wise warning for your credit's sake!
Which I for one failed not to take,
And hence could stem such strain and ache
    As each year might assign.

Standing by the Mantelpiece

(H.M.M., 1873)

This candle-wax is shaping to a shroud
To-night. (They call it that, as you may know) –
By touching it the claimant is avowed,
And hence I press it with my finger – so.

To-night. To me twice night, that should have been
The radiance of the midmost tick of noon,
And close around me wintertime is seen
That might have shone the veriest day of June!

But since all's lost, and nothing really lies
Above but shade, and shadier shade below,
Let me make clear, before one of us dies,
My mind to yours, just now embittered so.

Since you agreed, unurged and full-advised,
And let warmth grow without discouragement,
Why do you bear you now as if surprised,
When what has come was clearly consequent?

Since you have spoken, and finality
Closes around, and my last movements loom,
I say no more: the rest must wait till we
Are face to face again, yonside the tomb.

And let the candle-wax thus mould a shape
Whose meaning now, if hid before, you know,
And how by touch one present claims its drape,
And that it's I who press my finger – so.

That Kiss in the Dark

Recall it you? –
Say you do! –
When you went out into the night,
In an impatience that would not wait,
From that lone house in the woodland spot,
And when I, thinking you had gone
For ever and ever from my sight,
Came after, printing a kiss upon
Black air
In my despair,
And my two lips lit on your cheek
As you leant silent against a gate,
Making my woman's face flush hot
At what I had done in the dark, unware
You lingered for me but would not speak:
Yes, kissed you, thinking you were not there!
Recall it you? –
Say you do!

Suspense

A clamminess hangs over all like a clout,
The fields are a water-colour washed out,
The sky at its rim leaves a chink of light,
Like the lid of a pot that will not close tight.

She is away by the groaning sea,
Strained at the heart, and waiting for me:
Between us our foe from a hid retreat
Is watching, to wither us if we meet. . . .

But it matters little, however we fare –
Whether we meet, or I get not there;
The sky will look the same thereupon,
And the wind and the sea go groaning on.

The Musing Maiden

'Why so often, silent one,
Do you steal away alone?'
Starting, half she turned her head,
    And guiltily she said: –

'When the vane points to his far town
I go upon the hog-backed down,
And think the breeze that stroked his lip
    Over my own may slip.

'When he walks at close of day
I ramble on the white highway,
And think it reaches to his feet:
    A meditation sweet!

'When coasters hence to London sail
I watch their puffed wings waning pale;
His window opens near the quay;
    Their coming he can see.

'I go to meet the moon at night;
To mark the moon was our delight;
Up there our eyesights touch at will
    If such he practise still.'

W.P.V.
October 1866 (recopied)

A Daughter Returns

I like not that dainty-cut raiment, those earrings of pearl,
   I like not the light in that eye;
I like not the note of that voice. Never so was the girl
   Who a year ago bade me good-bye!

Hadst but come bare and moneyless, worn in the vamp, weather-
      gray,
   But innocent still as before,
How warmly I'd lodged thee! But sport thy new gains far away;
   I pray thee now – come here no more!

And yet I'll not try to blot out every memory of thee;
   I'll think of thee – yes, now and then:
One who's watched thee since Time called thee out o' thy mother
     and me
   Must think of thee; aye, I know when! . . .

When the cold sneer of dawn follows night-shadows black as a
      hearse,
   And the rain filters down the fruit tree,
And the tempest mouths into the flue-top a word like a curse,
   Then, then I shall think, think of thee!

17 December 1901

The Third Kissing-Gate

    She foots it forward down the town,
      Then leaves the lamps behind,
    And trots along the eastern road
      Where elms stand double-lined.

    She clacks the first dim kissing-gate
      Beneath the storm-strained trees,
    And passes to the second mead
      That fringes Mellstock Leaze.

She swings the second kissing-gate
   Next the gray garden-wall,
And sees the third mead stretching down
   Towards the waterfall.

And now the third-placed kissing-gate
   Her silent shadow nears,
And touches with; when suddenly
   Her person disappears.

What chanced by that third kissing-gate
   When the hushed mead grew dun?
Lo – two dark figures clasped and closed
   As if they were but one.

A Musical Incident

When I see the room it hurts me
   As with a pricking blade,
Those women being the memoried reason why my cheer deserts
    me. –
'Twas thus. One of them played
To please her friend, not knowing
That friend was speedily growing,
   Behind the player's chair,
   Somnolent, unaware
Of any music there.

I saw it, and it distressed me,
   For I had begun to think
I loved the drowsy listener, when this arose to test me
   And tug me from love's brink.
'Beautiful!' said she, waking
As the music ceased. 'Heart-aching!'
   Though never a note she'd heard
   To judge of as averred –
Save that of the very last word.

All would have faded in me,
   But that the sleeper brought

News a week thence that her friend was dead. It stirred within me
   Sense of injustice wrought
   That dead player's poor intent —
   So heartily, kindly meant —
   As blandly added the sigher:
   'How glad I am I was nigh her,
   To hear her last tune!' — 'Liar!'
   I lipped. — This gave love pause,
   And killed it, such as it was.

I Looked Back

I looked back as I left the house,
And, past the chimneys and neighbour tree,
The moon upsidled through the boughs: —
I thought: 'I shall a last time see
This picture; when will that time be?'

I paused amid the laugh-loud feast,
And selfward said: 'I am sitting where,
Some night, when ancient songs have ceased,
"Now is the last time I shall share
Such cheer," will be the thought I bear.'

An eye-sweep back at a look-out corner
Upon a hill, as forenight wore,
Stirred me to think: 'Ought I to warn her
That, though I come here times three-score,
One day 'twill be I come no more?'

Anon I reasoned there had been,
Ere quite forsaken was each spot,
Bygones whereon I'd lastly seen
That house, that feast, that maid forgot;
But when? — Ah, I remembered not!

Christmas: 1924

'Peace upon earth!' was said. We sing it,
And pay a million priests to bring it.
After two thousand years of mass
We've got as far as poison-gas.

1924

Dead 'Wessex' the Dog to the Household*

Do you think of me at all,
    Wistful ones?
Do you think of me at all
    As if nigh?
Do you think of me at all
At the creep of evenfall,
Or when the sky-birds call
    As they fly?

Do you look for me at times,
    Wistful ones?
Do you look for me at times
    Strained and still?
Do you look for me at times,
When the hour for walking chimes,
On that grassy path that climbs
    Up the hill?

You may hear a jump or trot,
    Wistful ones,
You may hear a jump or trot —
    Mine, as 'twere —
You may hear a jump or trot
On the stair or path or plot;
But I shall cause it not,
    Be not there.

Should you call as when I knew you,
    Wistful ones,

Should you call as when I knew you,
    Shared your home;
Should you call as when I knew you,
I shall not turn to view you,
I shall not listen to you,
    Shall not come.

Family Portraits

Three picture-drawn people stepped out of their frames –
    The blast, how it blew!
And the white-shrouded candles flapped smoke-headed flames;
– Three picture-drawn people came down from their frames,
And dumbly in lippings they told me their names,
    Full well though I knew.

The first was a maiden of mild wistful tone,
    Gone silent for years,
The next a dark woman in former time known;
But the first one, the maiden of mild wistful tone,
So wondering, unpractised, so vague and alone,
    Nigh moved me to tears.

The third was a sad man – a man of much gloom;
    And before me they passed
In the shade of the night, at the back of the room,
The dark and fair woman, the man of much gloom,
Three persons, in far-off years forceful, but whom
    Death now fettered fast.

They set about acting some drama, obscure,
    The women and he,
With puppet-like movements of mute strange allure;
Yea, set about acting some drama, obscure,
Till I saw 'twas their own lifetime's tragic amour,
    Whose course begot me;

Yea – a mystery, ancestral, long hid from my reach
    In the perished years past,
That had mounted to dark doings each against each

In those ancestors' days, and long hid from my reach;
Which their restless enghostings, it seemed, were to teach
    Me in full, at this last.

But fear fell upon me like frost, of some hurt
    If they entered anew
On the orbits they smartly had swept when expert
In the law-lacking passions of life, – of some hurt
To their souls – and thus mine – which I fain would avert;
    So, in sweat cold as dew,

'Why wake up all this?' I cried out. 'Now, so late!
    Let old ghosts be laid!'
And they stiffened, drew back to their frames and numb state,
Gibbering: 'Thus are your own ways to shape, know too late!'
Then I grieved that I'd not had the courage to wait
    And see the play played.

I have grieved ever since: to have balked future pain,
    My blood's tendance foreknown,
Had been triumph. Nights long stretched awake I have lain
Perplexed in endeavours to balk future pain
By uncovering the drift of their drama. In vain,
    Though therein lay my own.

A Private Man on Public Men

When my contemporaries were driving
Their coach through Life with strain and striving,
And raking riches into heaps,
And ably pleading in the Courts
With smart rejoinders and retorts,
Or where the Senate nightly keeps
Its vigils, till their fames were fanned
By rumour's tongue throughout the land,
I lived in quiet, screened, unknown,
Pondering upon some stick or stone,
Or news of some rare book or bird
Latterly bought, or seen, or heard,
Not wishing ever to set eyes on

The surging crowd beyond the horizon,
Tasting years of moderate gladness
Mellowed by sundry days of sadness,
Shut from the noise of the world without,
Hearing but dimly its rush and rout,
Unenvying those amid its roar,
Little endowed, not wanting more.

He Resolves to Say No More*

O my soul, keep the rest unknown!
It is too like a sound of moan
        When the charnel-eyed
        Pale Horse has nighed:
Yea, none shall gather what I hide!

Why load men's minds with more to bear
That bear already ails to spare?
        From now alway
        Till my last day
What I discern I will not say.

Let Time roll backward if it will;
(Magians who drive the midnight quill
        With brain aglow
        Can see it so,)
What I have learnt no man shall know.

And if my vision range beyond
The blinkered sight of souls in bond,
        — By truth made free —
        I'll let all be,
And show to no man what I see.

from
UNCOLLECTED POEMS

Domicilium*

It faces west, and round the back and sides
High beeches, bending, hang a veil of boughs,
And sweep against the roof. Wild honeysucks
Climb on the walls, and seem to sprout a wish
(If we may fancy wish of trees and plants)
To overtop the apple-trees hard by.

Red roses, lilacs, variegated box
Are there in plenty, and such hardy flowers
As flourish best untrained. Adjoining these
Are herbs and esculents; and farther still
A field; then cottages with trees, and last
The distant hills and sky.

Behind, the scene is wilder. Heath and furze
Are everything that seems to grow and thrive
Upon the uneven ground. A stunted thorn
Stands here and there, indeed; and from a pit
An oak uprises, springing from a seed
Dropped by some bird a hundred years ago.

                In days bygone –
Long gone – my father's mother, who is now
Blest with the blest, would take me out to walk.
At such a time I once inquired of her
How looked the spot when first she settled here.
The answer I remember. 'Fifty years
Have passed since then, my child, and change has marked
The face of all things. Yonder garden-plots
And orchards were uncultivated slopes
O'ergrown with bramble bushes, furze and thorn:
That road a narrow path shut in by ferns,
Which, almost trees, obscured the passer-by.

On the Doorstep*

She sits in her night-dress without the door,
And her father comes up: 'He at it again?'
He mournfully cries. 'Poor girlie!' and then
Comes her husband to fetch her in, shamed and sore.
The elder strikes him. He falls head-bare
On the edge of the step, and lies senseless there.

She, seeing him stretched like a corpse at length,
Cries out to her father, who stands aghast,
'I hate you with all my soul and strength!
You've killed him. And if this word's my last
I hate you. . . . O my husband dear –
Live – do as you will! None shall interfere!'

from THE DYNASTS

The Night of Trafalgár*
(*Boatman's Song*)

i

In the wild October night-time, when the wind raved round the
land,
And the Back-sea met the Front-sea, and our doors were blocked
with sand,
And we heard the drub of Dead-man's Bay, where bones of
thousands are,
We knew not what the day had done for us at Trafalgár.
                    Had done,
                    Had done,
            For us at Trafalgár!

ii

'Pull hard, and make the Nothe, or down we go!' one says, says he.
We pulled; and bedtime brought the storm; but snug at home slept
we.

Yet all the while our gallants after fighting through the day,
Were beating up and down the dark, sou'-west of Cadiz Bay.

The dark,
The dark,
Sou'-west of Cadiz Bay!

iii

The victors and the vanquished then the storm it tossed and tore,
As hard they strove, those worn-out men, upon that surly shore;
Dead Nelson and his half-dead crew, his foes from near and far,
Were rolled together on the deep that night at Trafalgár!

The deep,
The deep,
That night at Trafalgár!

Budmouth Dears*

(Hussar's Song)

i

When we lay where Budmouth Beach is,
O, the girls were fresh as peaches,
With their tall and tossing figures and their eyes of blue and
brown!
And our hearts would ache with longing
As we paced from our sing-songing,
With a smart *Clink! Clink!* up the Esplanade and down.

ii

They distracted and delayed us
By the pleasant pranks they played us,
And what marvel, then, if troopers, even of regiments of renown,
On whom flashed those eyes divine, O,
Should forget the countersign, O,
As we tore *Clink! Clink!* back to camp above the town.

iii

Do they miss us much, I wonder,
Now that war has swept us sunder,

And we roam from where the faces smile to where the faces
     frown?
    And no more behold the features
    Of the fair fantastic creatures,
And no more *Clink! Clink!* past the parlours of the town?

          iv
    Shall we once again there meet them?
    Falter fond attempts to greet them?
Will the gay sling-jacket glow again beside the muslin gown? —
    Will they archly quiz and con us
    With a sideway glance upon us,
While our spurs *Clink! Clink!* up the Esplanade and down?

*The Eve of Waterloo**

(*Chorus of Phantoms*)

The eyelids of eve fall together at last,
And the forms so foreign to field and tree
Lie down as though native, and slumber fast!

Sore are the thrills of misgiving we see
In the artless champaign at this harlequinade,
Distracting a vigil where calm should be!

The green seems opprest, and the Plain afraid
Of a Something to come, whereof these are the proofs, —
Neither earthquake, nor storm, nor eclipse's shade!

Yea, the coneys are scared by the thud of hoofs,
And their white scuts flash at their vanishing heels,
And swallows abandon the hamlet-roofs.

The mole's tunnelled chambers are crushed by wheels,
The lark's eggs scattered, their owners fled;
And the hedgehog's household the sapper unseals.

The snail draws in at the terrible tread,
But in vain; he is crushed by the felloe-rim;
The worm asks what can be overheard,

And wriggles deep from a scene so grim,
And guesses him safe; for he does not know
What a foul red flood will be soaking him!

Beaten about by the heel and toe
Are butterflies, sick of the day's long rheum
To die of a worse than the weather-foe.

Trodden and bruised to a miry tomb
Are ears that have greened but will never be gold,
And flowers in the bud that will never bloom.

So the season's intent, ere its fruit unfold,
Is frustrate, and mangled, and made succumb,
Like a youth of promise struck stark and cold! . . .

And what of these who to-night have come?
The young sleep sound; but the weather awakes
In the veterans, pains from the past that numb;

Old stabs of Ind, old Peninsular aches,
Old Friedland chills, haunt their moist mud bed,
Cramps from Austerlitz; till their slumber breaks.

And each soul shivers as sinks his head
On the loam he's to lease with the other dead
From tomorrow's mist-fall till Time be sped!

APPENDIX:
HARDY'S PREFACES AND APOLOGY

PREFACE TO
WESSEX POEMS AND OTHER VERSES

Of the miscellaneous collection of verse that follows, only four pieces have been published, though many were written long ago, and others partly written. In some few cases the verses were turned into prose and printed as such, it having been unanticipated at that time that they might see the light.

Whenever an ancient and legitimate word of the district, for which there was no equivalent in received English, suggested itself as the most natural, nearest, and often only expression of a thought, it has been made use of, on what seemed good grounds.

The pieces are in a large degree dramatic or personative in conception; and this even where they are not obviously so.

The dates attached to some of the poems do not apply to the rough sketches given in illustration,[1] which have been recently made, and, as may be surmised, are inserted for personal and local reasons rather than for their intrinsic qualities.

September 1898   T.H.

[1] The early editions were illustrated by the author.

PREFACE TO
POEMS OF THE PAST AND THE PRESENT

Herewith I tender my thanks to the editors and proprietors of *The Times*, the *Morning Post*, the *Daily Chronicle*, the *Westminster Gazette*, *Literature*, the *Graphic*, *Cornhill*, *Sphere*, and other papers, for permission to reprint from their pages such of the following pieces of verse as have already been published.

Of the subject-matter of this volume — even that which is in other than narrative form — much is dramatic or impersonative even where not explicitly so. Moreover, that portion which may be regarded as individual comprises a series of feelings and fancies written down in widely differing moods and circumstances, and at various dates. It will probably be found, therefore, to possess little cohesion of thought or harmony of colouring. I do not greatly regret this. Unadjusted impressions have their value, and the road to a true philosophy of life seems to lie in humbly recording diverse readings of its phenomena as they are forced upon us by chance and change.

August 1901   T.H.

PREFACE TO
TIME'S LAUGHINGSTOCKS AND OTHER VERSES

In collecting the following poems I have to thank the editors and proprietors of the periodicals in which certain of them have appeared for permission to reclaim them.

Now that the miscellany is brought together, some lack of concord in pieces written at widely severed dates, and in contrasting moods and circumstances, will be obvious enough. This I cannot help, but the sense of disconnection, particularly in respect of those lyrics penned in the first person, will be immaterial when it is borne in mind that they are to be regarded, in the main, as dramatic monologues by different characters.

As a whole they will, I hope, take the reader forward, even if not far, rather than backward. I should add that some lines in the early-dated poems have been rewritten, though they have been left substantially unchanged.

September 1909   T.H.

APOLOGY FROM
LATE LYRICS AND EARLIER*

About half the verses that follow were written quite lately. The rest are older, having been held over in MS. when past volumes were published, on considering that these would contain a sufficient number of pages to offer readers at one time, more especially during the distractions of the war. The unusually far back poems to be found here are, however, but some that were overlooked in gathering previous collections. A freshness in them, now unattainable, seemed to make up for their inexperience and to justify their inclusion. A few are dated; the dates of others are not discoverable.

The launching of a volume of this kind in neo-Georgian days by one who began writing in mid-Victorian, and has published nothing to speak of for some years, may seem to call for a few words of excuse or explanation. Whether or no, readers may feel assured that a new book is submitted to them with great hesitation at so belated a date. Insistent practical reasons, however, among which were requests from some illustrious men of letters who are in sympathy with my productions, the accident that several of the poems have already seen the light, and that dozens of them have been lying about for years, compelled the course adopted, in spite of the natural disinclination of a writer whose works have been so frequently regarded askance by a pragmatic section here and there, to draw attention to them once more.

I do not know that it is necessary to say much on the contents of the book, even in deference to suggestions that will be mentioned presently. I believe that those readers who care for my poems at all – readers to whom no passport is required – will care for this new instalment of them, perhaps the last, as much as for any that have preceded them. Moreover, in the eyes of a less friendly class the pieces, though a very mixed collection indeed, contain, so far as I am able to see, little or nothing in technic or teaching that can be considered a Star-Chamber matter, or so much as agitating to a ladies' school; even though, to use Wordsworth's observation in his Preface to *Lyrical Ballads*, such readers may suppose 'that by the act of writing in verse an author makes a formal engagement that he will gratify certain known habits of association: that he not only thus apprises the reader that certain classes of ideas and expressions will be found in his book, but that others will be carefully excluded.'

It is true, nevertheless, that some grave, positive, stark, delineations are interspersed among those of the passive, lighter, and traditional sort presumably nearer to stereotyped tastes. For – while I am quite aware that a thinker is not expected, and, indeed, is scarcely allowed, now more than heretofore, to state all that crosses his mind concerning existence in this universe, in his attempts to explain or excuse the presence of evil and the incongruity of penalizing the irresponsible – it must be obvious to open intelligences that, without denying the beauty and faithful service of certain venerable cults, such disallowance of 'obstinate questionings' and 'blank misgivings' tends to a para-lysed intellectual stalemate. Heine observed nearly a hundred years ago that the soul has her eternal rights; that she will not be darkened by statutes, nor lullabied by the music of bells. And what is to-day, in allusions to the present author's pages, alleged to be 'pessimism' is, in truth, only such 'questionings' in the exploration of reality, and is the first step towards the soul's betterment, and the body's also.

If I may be forgiven for quoting my own old words, let me repeat what I printed in this relation more than twenty years ago, and wrote much earlier, in a poem entitled 'In Tenebris':

If way to the Better there be, it exacts a full look at the Worst:

that is to say, by the exploration of reality, and its frank recognition stage by stage along the survey, with an eye to the best consummation possible: briefly, evolutionary meliorism. But it is called pessimism nevertheless; under which word, expressed with condemnatory emphasis, it is regarded by many as some pernicious new thing (though so old as to underlie the Gospel scheme, and even to permeate the Greek drama); and the subject is charitably left to decent silence, as if further comment were needless.

Happily there are some who feel such Levitical passing-by to be, alas, by no means a permanent dismissal of the matter; that comment on where the world stands is very much the reverse of needless in these disordered years of our prematurely afflicted century: that amendment and not madness lies that way. And looking down the future these few hold fast to the same: that whether the human and kindred animal races survive till the exhaustion or destruction of the globe, or whether these races perish and are succeeded by others before that conclusion comes, pain to all upon it, tongued or dumb, shall be kept down to a minimum by loving-kindness, operating through scientific knowledge, and actuated by the modicum of free will conjecturally possessed by organic life when the mighty necessitating forces – unconscious or other – that have 'the balancings of the clouds', happen to be in equilibrium, which may or may not be often.

To conclude this question I may add that the argument of the so-called optimists is neatly summarized in a stern pronouncement against me by my friend Mr Frederic Harrison in a late essay of his, in the words: 'This view of life is not mine.' The solemn declaration does not seem to me to be so annihilating to the said 'view' (really a series of fugitive impressions which I have never tried to co-ordinate) as is complacently assumed. Surely it embodies a too human fallacy quite familiar in logic. Next, a knowing reviewer, apparently a Roman Catholic young man, speaks, with some rather gross instances of the *suggestio falsi* in his whole article, of 'Mr Hardy refusing consolation', the 'dark gravity of his ideas', and so on. When a Positivist and a Romanist agree there must be something wonderful in it, which should make a poet sit up. But . . . O that 'twere possible!

I would not have alluded in this place or anywhere else to such casual personal criticisms – for casual and unreflecting they must be – but for the satisfaction of two or three friends in whose opinion a short answer was deemed desirable, on account of the continual repetition of these criticisms, or more precisely, quizzings. After all, the serious and truly literary inquiry in this connection is: Should a shaper of such stuff as dreams are made on disregard considerations of what is customary and expected, and apply himself to the real function of poetry, the application of ideas to life (in Matthew Arnold's familiar phrase)? This bears more particularly on what has been called the 'philosophy' of these poems – usually reproved as 'queer'. Whoever the author may be that undertakes such application of ideas in this 'philosophic' direction – where it is specially required – glacial judgments must inevitably fall upon him amid opinion whose arbiters largely decry individuality, to whom *ideas* are oddities to smile at, who are moved by a yearning the reverse of that of the Athenian inquirers on Mars Hill; and stiffen their features not only at sound of a new thing, but at a restatement of old things in new terms. Hence should anything of this sort in the following adumbrations seem 'queer' – should any of them seem to good Panglossians to embody strange and disrespectful conceptions of this best of all possible worlds, I apologize; but cannot help it.

Such divergences, which, though piquant for the nonce, it would be affectation to say are not saddening and discouraging likewise, may, to be sure, arise sometimes from superficial aspect only, writer and reader seeing the same thing at different angles. But in palpable cases of divergence they arise, as already said, whenever a serious effort is made towards that which the authority I have cited – who would now be called old-fashioned, possibly even parochial – affirmed to be what no good critic could deny as the poet's province, the application of ideas to life. One might shrewdly guess, by the by, that in such recommendation the famous writer may have overlooked the cold-shouldering results upon an enthusiastic disciple that would be pretty certain to follow his putting the high aim in practice, and have forgotten the disconcerting experience of Gil Blas with the Archbishop.

To add a few more words to what has already taken up too many, there is a contingency liable to miscellanies of verse that I have never seen mentioned, so far as I can remember; I mean the chance little shocks that may be caused over a book of various character like the present and its predecessors by the juxtaposition of unrelated, even discordant, effusions; poems perhaps years apart in the making, yet facing each other. An odd result of this has been that dramatic anecdotes of a satirical and humorous intention following verse in graver voice, have been read as misfires because they raise the smile that they were intended to raise, the journalist, deaf to the sudden change of key, being unconscious that he is laughing with the author and not at him. I admit that I did not foresee such contingencies as I ought to have done, and that people might not perceive when the tone altered. But the difficulties of arranging the themes in a graduated kinship of moods would have been so great that irrelation was almost unavoidable with efforts so diverse. I must trust for right note-catching to those finely-touched spirits who can divine without half a whisper, whose intuitiveness is proof against all the accidents of inconsequence. In respect of the less alert, however, should any one's train of thought be thrown out of gear by a consecutive piping of vocal reeds in jarring tonics, without a semiquaver's rest between, and be led thereby to miss the writer's aim and meaning in one out of two contiguous compositions, I shall deeply regret it.

Having at last, I think, finished with the personal points that I was recommended to notice, I will forsake the immediate object of this Preface; and, leaving *Late Lyrics* to whatever fate it deserves, digress for a few moments to more general considerations. The thoughts of any man of letters concerned to keep poetry alive cannot but run uncomfortably on the precarious prospects of English verse at the present day. Verily the hazards and casualties surrounding the birth and setting forth of almost every modern creation in numbers are ominously like those of one of Shelley's paper-boats on a windy lake. And a forward conjecture scarcely permits the hope of a better time, unless men's tendencies should change. So indeed of all art, literature, and 'high thinking' nowadays. Whether owing to the barbarizing of taste in the younger minds by the dark madness of the late war, the unabashed cultivation of selfishness in all classes, the plethoric growth of knowledge simultaneously with the stunting of wisdom, 'a degrading thirst after outrageous stimulation' (to quote Wordsworth again), or from any other cause, we seem threatened with a new Dark Age.

I formerly thought, like other much exercised writers, that so far as literature was concerned a partial cause might be impotent or mischievous criticism; the satirizing of individuality, the lack of whole-seeing in contemporary estimates of poetry and kindred work, the knowingness affected by junior reviewers, the overgrowth of meticulousness in their peerings for an opinion, as if it were a cultivated habit in them to scrutinize the tool-marks and be blind to the building, to hearken for the key-creaks and be deaf to the diapason, to judge the landscape by a nocturnal exploration with a flash-lantern. In other words, to carry on the old game of sampling the poem or drama by quoting the worst line or worst passage only, in ignorance or not of Coleridge's proof that a versification of any length neither can be nor ought to be all poetry; of reading meanings into a book that its author never dreamt of writing there. I might go on interminably.

But I do not now think any such temporary obstructions to be the cause of the hazard, for these negligences and ignorances, though they may have stifled a few true poets in the run of generations, disperse like stricken leaves before the wind of next week, and are no more heard of again in the region of letters than their writers themselves. No: we may be convinced that something of the deeper sort mentioned must be the cause.

In any event poetry, pure literature in general, religion – I include religion, in its essential and undogmatic sense, because poetry and religion touch each other, or rather modulate into each other; are, indeed, often but different names for the same thing – these, I say, the visible signs of mental and emotional life, must like all other things keep moving, becoming; even though at present, when belief in witches of Endor is displacing the Darwinian theory and 'the truth that shall make you free', men's minds appear, as above noted, to be moving backwards rather than on. I speak somewhat sweepingly, and should except many thoughtful writers in verse and prose; also men in certain worthy but small bodies of various denominations, and perhaps in the homely quarter where advance might have been the very least expected a few years back – the English Church – if one reads it rightly as showing evidence of 'removing those things that are shaken', in accordance with the wise Epistolary recommendation to the Hebrews. For since the historic and once august hierarchy of Rome some generation ago lost its chance of being the religion of the future by doing otherwise, and throwing over the little band of New Catholics who were making a struggle for continuity by applying the principle of evolution to their own faith, joining hands with modern science, and outflanking the hesitating English instinct towards liturgical restatement (a flank march which I at the time quite expected to witness, with the gathering of many millions of waiting agnostics into its fold); since then, one may ask, what other purely English establishment than the Church, of sufficient dignity and footing, with such strength of old association, such scope for transmutability, such architectural spell, is left in this country to keep the shreds of morality together?[1]

It may indeed be a forlorn hope, a mere dream, that of an alliance between religion, which must be retained unless the world is to perish, and complete rationality, which must come, unless also the world is to perish, by means of the interfusing effect of poetry – 'the breath and finer spirit of all knowledge; the impassioned expression of science', as it was defined by an English poet who was quite orthodox in his ideas. But if it be true, as Comte argued, that advance is never in a straight line, but in a looped orbit, we may, in the aforesaid ominous moving backward, be doing it *pour mieux sauter*, drawing back for a spring. I repeat that I forlornly hope so, notwithstanding the supercilious regard of hope by Schopenhauer, von Hartmann, and other philosophers down to Einstein who have my respect. But one dares not prophesy. Physical, chronological, and other contingencies keep me in these days from critical studies and literary circles

> Where once we held debate, a band
> Of youthful friends, on mind and art

(if one may quote Tennyson in this century). Hence I cannot know how things are going so well as I used to know them, and the aforesaid limitations must quite prevent my knowing henceforward.

I have to thank the editors and owners of *The Times*, *Fortnightly*, *Mercury*, and other periodicals in which a few of the poems have appeared for kindly assenting to their being reclaimed for collected publication.

February 1922   T.H.

[1] However, one must not be too sanguine in reading signs, and since the above was written evidence that the Church will go far in the removal of 'things that are shaken' has not been encouraging.

INTRODUCTORY NOTE TO
WINTER WORDS IN VARIOUS MOODS
AND METRES

So far as I am aware, I happen to be the only English poet who has brought out a new volume of his verse on his . . . birthday,* whatever may have been the case with the ancient Greeks, for it must be remembered that poets did not die young in those days.

This, however, is not the point of the present few preliminary words. My last volume of poems was pronounced wholly gloomy and pessimistic by reviewers – even by some of the more able class. My sense of the oddity of this verdict may be imagined when, in selecting them, I had been, as I thought, rather too liberal in admitting flippant, not to say farcical, pieces into the collection. However, I did not suppose that the licensed tasters had wilfully misrepresented the book, and said nothing, knowing well that they could not have read it.

As labels stick, I foresee readily enough that the same perennial inscription will be set on the following pages, and therefore take no trouble to argue on the proceeding, notwithstanding the surprises to which I could treat my critics by uncovering a place here and there to them in the volume.

This being probably my last appearance on the literary stage, I would say, more seriously, that though, alas, it would be idle to pretend that the publication of these poems can have much interest for me, the track having been adventured so many times before to-day, the pieces themselves have been prepared with reasonable care, if not quite with the zest of a young man new to print.

I also repeat what I have often stated on such occasions, that no harmonious philosophy is attempted in these pages – or in any bygone pages of mine, for that matter.

T.H.

NOTES

ABBREVIATIONS

EL: Florence Emily Hardy, *The Early Life of Thomas Hardy* (London, 1928).

H: *The Complete Poetical Works of Thomas Hardy*, Volume I, ed. Samuel Hynes (Oxford, 1982).

JG: *Thomas Hardy: The Complete Poems*, ed. James Gibson (London, 1976, reissued with corrections, 1978).

Letters: The Collected Letters of Thomas Hardy, eds Richard Little Purdy and Michael Millgate (Oxford, 1982).

LY: Florence Emily Hardy, *The Later Years of Thomas Hardy* (London, 1930).

Orel: *Thomas Hardy's Personal Writings*, ed. Harold Orel (London, 1967).

ORFW: *One Rare Fair Woman: Thomas Hardy's Letters to Florence Henniker*, eds Evelyn Hardy and F. B. Pinion (London, 1972).

Purdy: *Thomas Hardy: A Bibliographical Study* by Richard Little Purdy (Oxford, 1954, reissued 1978).

SCC: *Friends of a Lifetime: Letters to Sydney Carlyle Cockerell*, ed. Viola Meynell (London, 1940).

SP: *Selected Poems of Thomas Hardy* (London, 1916).

WESSEX POEMS AND OTHER VERSES (pp. 1–18)

First published in December 1898; manuscript, which also contains thirty-two original drawings, in the Birmingham City Museum and Art Gallery.

p. 3 'Postponement': H (p. 361) draws attention to the following exchange in *Talks with Thomas Hardy at Max Gate: 1920–1922* by Vere H. Collins (London, 1928):

> C: I am not clear what is the human application of the last stanza – 'Ah, had I been . . . born to an evergreen nesting-tree.'
> H: You see, earlier in the poem the young man is described as not being able to marry for want of money; and the woman as not waiting, but marrying someone else.
> C: I understand that. The 'being born to an evergreen tree' means, then, simply, and solely having money?
> H: Yes.

p. 4 'Neutral Tones': in *SP* the poem ends with [written at] 'Westbourne Park Villas'.

p. 4 'She at His Funeral': 'A Chronological List of Thomas Hardy's Works' dates this poem 1873.

p. 5 'She to Him I': one of a series of four sonnets, printed on its own here even though Hardy told his publisher Macmillan (24 March 1925): 'The four "She, to Him" sonnets [are] to be reckoned as one poem, which they are' (H, pp. 362–3).

p. 5 'Valenciennes': the same story is told, briefly, by Corporal Tullidge in *The Trumpet-Major*, Ch. IV. A-topperèn: knocking on the head; slent to shards: blown to bits.

p. 7 'Her Death and After': Hardy reckoned this poem and 'The Dance at the Phoenix' 'as good stories as I have ever told' (*Letters* II, p. 283).

p. 13 'The Ivy-Wife': Emma, Hardy's first wife, took the poem personally (H, p. 364).

p. 14 'Friends Beyond': a number of these names also appear elsewhere in Hardy, e.g. William Dewy in *Under the Greenwood Tree*; Lady Susan's story is also told in *EL*. Mellstock: Stinsford.

p. 15 'Thoughts of Phena': 'Phena' was Hardy's cousin, Tryphena Sparks (1851–1890), whose life may also have given Hardy some material for Sue Bridehead in *Jude the Obscure*, and for the poem 'My Cecily'. *SP* title: 'At News of a Woman's Death'. In *EL* (p. 293) we find an extract from Hardy's diary for 5 March 1890: 'In the train on the way to London. Wrote the first four or six lines of "Not a line of her writing have I". It was a curious instance of sympathetic telepathy. The woman I was thinking of – a cousin – was dying at the time, and I was quite in ignorance of it. She died six days later. The remainder of the piece was not written till after her death.' **nimb**: nimbus.

p. 16 'Nature's Questioning': Hardy wrote to Alfred Noyes about this poem, saying that its 'definitions' – such as 'some Vast Imbecility' – 'are merely enumerated in the poem as fanciful alternatives to several others, and have nothing to do with my own opinion' (H, p. 365).

p. 17 'In a Eweleaze near Weatherbury': **Weatherbury**: Puddletown.

p. 18 'I Look Into My Glass': a similar thought occurs in Hardy's diary for December 1892 (see *LY*, pp. 13–14), and in *The Well-Beloved*, Part II, Ch. XII.

POEMS OF THE PAST AND THE PRESENT (pp. 19–39)

First published 17 December 1901; holograph of manuscript in the Bodleian Library, Oxford.

p. 21 'Drummer Hodge': the poem refers to the Boer War (1899–1902), and was originally published as 'The Dead Drummer'. Hardy gave his views on the name 'Hodge' in *Tess of the d'Urbervilles* (Ch. XVIII) and in his essay 'The Dorsetshire Labourer' (Orel, pp. 168–89).

p. 21 'A Wife in London': the poem was originally written in the first person.

p. 22 *Poems of Pilgrimage*: Hardy and Emma visited Italy in March and April 1887, and Switzerland in June and July 1897.

p. 22 'Shelley's Skylark': Shelley wrote 'To a Skylark' in Leghorn in June 1820.

p. 26 'To an Unborn Pauper Child': JG records MS note after title: 'She must go to the Union-house to have her baby. *Petty Sessions*.'

p. 27 'To Lizbie Browne': 'Lizbie Browne was a red-haired game-keeper's daughter, a year or two older than Hardy' (H, p. 372).

p. 29 'The Well-Beloved': the poem is set at Jourdan Hill, near Weymouth, on the site of the Roman 'Clavinium'. **Ikling Way**: also Icen or Icening Way; **Kingsbere**: Bere Regis.

p. 31 'A Broken Appointment': Purdy (p. 113) links the poem to Mrs Henniker, and suggests the setting is the British Museum.

p. 35 'The Darkling Thrush': first published in the *Graphic* (29 December 1900) as 'By the Century's Deathbed'. H and others suggest a possible source in W. H. Hudson's *Nature in Downland* (London, 1900, pp. 249–52).

p. 37 'The Ruined Maid': 'barton: farmyard; megrims: migraines.

p. 37 'The Self-Unseeing': originally entitled 'Unregarding'. former door: during Hardy's lifetime, the front door of the house in which he had been born was moved from its original position.

p. 38 In Tenebris 1: one of a series of three poems. Epitaph is from Psalm 101, verse 5 in the Vulgate. The Authorized Version (Psalm 102, verse 4) reads: 'My heart is smitten, and withered like grass.'

TIME'S LAUGHINGSTOCKS AND OTHER VERSES (pp. 41–69)

First published 3 December 1909; manuscript in the Fitzwilliam Museum, Cambridge.

p. 43 'A Trampwoman's Tragedy': 'Hardy considered this, upon the whole, his most successful poem' (*EL*, p. 311). JG points out that MS has '1827' for '182–'. H (p. 380) quotes Hardy to Gosse, 15 November 1903: 'It was written between one and two years ago, after a bicycle journey I took across the Poldon Hill described, and on to Glastonbury. I wish you could see the view from the top. "Marshal's Elm" you will find on any map of Somerset. The circumstances have been known to me for many years. You may like to be told that the woman's name was Mary Ann Taylor – though she has been dust for half a century.'

p. 46 'A Sunday Morning Tragedy': in 1909 the poem was rejected by the *Fortnightly Review* on the grounds that the magazine 'circulates among families' (H, p. 382).

p. 50 'The Curate's Kindness': Union: the Union of Boards of the Guardians of the Poor.

p. 52 'Shut Out That Moon': Lady's Chair is the constellation Cassiopeia.

p. 53 'The Dead Man Walking': JG points out that the MS adds '1896'.

p. 58 'He Abjures Love': in a letter to Alfred Noyes Hardy insisted that this poem 'is a love-poem, and the lovers are chartered impossibilities' (*LY*, p. 218).

p. 59 'At Casterbridge Fair': there are seven songs in this series. Casterbridge: Dorchester.

p. 60 'After the Fair': JG points out the MS note: '"The chimes" will be listened for in vain here at midnight now, having been abolished some years ago.'

p. 65 'After the Last Breath': Jemima Hardy, Hardy's mother, died 3 April 1904.

p. 67 'One We Knew': M.H. stands for Mary Hardy, Hardy's grandmother.

p. 68 'The Unborn': first published as 'Life's Opportunity'. It seems likely that '1905' refers to the date of revision rather than composition.

p. 69 'The Man He Killed': nipperkin: half-pint measure.

SATIRES OF CIRCUMSTANCE: LYRICS AND REVERIES
(pp. 71–118)

First published 17 November 1914; manuscript in the Dorset County Museum.

p. 75 'Channel Firing': this poem refers to gunnery practice on the south coast on the eve of the First World War; it was published four months before war broke out. **glebe**: parson's field.

p. 76 'The Convergence of the Twain': the SS *Titanic* was sunk by an iceberg during its maiden voyage on 15 April 1912; Hardy's poem was first published the following month in the souvenir programme of an event organized to raise money for the victims.

p. 77 'After the Visit': F.E.D. stands for Florence Emily Dugdale, Hardy's second wife, whom he married in 1914.

p. 78 'When I Set Out for Lyonnesse': Lyonnesse is the north Cornwall of Arthurian legend. Hardy met his first wife, Emma, at St Juliot in Cornwall in 1870.

p. 79 'Beyond the Last Lamp': Hardy lived in Tooting, south London, from 1878 to 1881. The poem was originally called 'Night in a Suburb'.

p. 82 'The Place on the Map': the poem originally had the subtitle 'A Poor Schoolmaster's Story'.

p. 83 'God's Funeral': the poem originally had the subtitle 'An Allegorical Conception/Of the Present State of Theology'.

p. 89 _Poems of 1912–13_: Emma, Hardy's first wife, died on 27 November 1912, and the following March Hardy visited Cornwall, where they had met and courted in the early 1970s. _Veteris vestigia flammae_: traces of the old flame (Virgil, _Aeneid_, IV, 23).

p. 93 'I Found Her Out There': _SP_ ends 'December 1912'.

p. 97 'The Voice': JG records, among other small MS variations: l. 11 'consigned to existlessness' for 'dissolved to wan wistlessness'. Hardy reports the meeting described in stanza two in _EL_, p. 103. Wistlessness: unknowingness.

p. 101 'Beeny Cliff': in his diary for 10 March 1870, Hardy has 'Went with E.L.G. to Beeny Cliff. She on horseback . . . On the cliff . . . "The tender grace of a day", etc. The run down to the edge. The coming home' (_EL_, p. 99). **irised**: made iridescent.

p. 105 'The Spell of the Rose': in the MS this poem was printed after 'Under the Waterfall'.

p. 106 'St Launce's Revisited': in the MS this poem was printed after 'The Spell of the Rose' and before 'The Going'.

p. 116 'Exeunt Omnes': on 2 June 1913 Hardy was seventy-three; it was his first birthday since Emma's death. **Kennels**: gutters.

p. 117 _Satires of Circumstance_: when this series of fifteen poems was first published in 1911, Hardy wrote to Mrs Henniker (_ORFW_, p. 146): 'You will remember, I am sure, that being _satires_ they are rather brutal. I express no feeling or opinion myself at all. They are from notes I made some twenty years ago, and then found were more fit for verse than prose.'

MOMENTS OF VISION AND MISCELLANEOUS VERSES
(pp. 119–52)

First published 30 November 1917; manuscript in the Old Library of Magdalene College, Cambridge.

p. 121 'We Sat at the Window': the poem remembers a visit that Hardy and Emma made to Bournemouth in 1875. Traditionally, rain on St Swithin's Day, 15 July, means the next forty days will be wet.

p. 122 'At the Word "Farewell"': *EL*, p. 99, also describes Hardy's parting from Emma after his first visit to Cornwall in 1870. JG points out MS has, at the end, cancelled '1913'.

p. 123 'First Sight of Her and After': *SP* links this poem to 'At the Word "Farewell"' by its having the cancelled title 'The Return from First Beholding Her'.

p. 124 'Near Lanivet, 1872': *ORFW*, p. 179, makes it clear this poem remembers an actual incident.

p. 125 'Quid Hic Agis?': the title is from the Vulgate text of I Kings, 19:9. In the Authorized Version it reads 'What dost thou here?'

p. 127 'The Blinded Bird': ll. 15–20 refer to I Corinthians 13:4–7.

p. 132 'The Oxen': first published in *The Times*, 24 December 1915. See also *Tess*, Ch. XVII.

p. 134 'The Last Signal': William Barnes (1801–1886), the dialect poet, was Hardy's friend and – for several years – neighbour. After his death, Hardy edited a selection of his poems. See also *EL*, p. 240.

p. 136 'Overlooking the River Stour': JG points out that the MS has deleted beneath the title: '(1877)'. Hardy and Emma lived at Sturminster Newton, on the River Stour, from July 1876 to March 1878, and later referred to this time as an 'idyll . . . Our happiest time'.

p. 138 'The Interloper': l. 31 refers to Daniel 3:45.

p. 139 'Logs on the Hearth': Mary Hardy, Hardy's sister, died on 24 November 1915. See also 'Molly Gone', 'In the Garden' and 'The Sun's Last Look on the Country Girl'.

p. 143 'I Thought, My Heart': in the MS of *Moments of Vision* Hardy added a third verse, which also appears in Ruth Head's *Pages from the Works of Thomas Hardy* (1922):

> That kiss so strange, so stark, I'll take
> When the world sleeps sound, and no noise will scare,
> And a moon-touch whitens each stone and stake;
>   Yes; I will meet her there –
> Just at the time she calls '*to-morrow*',
> But I call '*after the shut of sorrow*' –
>   And with her dwell –
>   Inseparable

> With cease of pain,
> And frost and rain,
> And life's inane.

p. 144 'Midnight on the Great Western': see also *Jude the Obscure*, V, III.

p. 145 'The Clock-Winder': ll. 29–44 do not appear in the MS.

p. 147 'The Choirmaster's Burial': Thomas Hardy, Hardy's grandfather, sang in Stinsford Church choir and was buried in 1837.

p. 149 'Men Who March Away': the poem is set at the County Hall, Dorchester, in 1914.

p. 150 'In Time of "The Breaking of Nations"': the reference to Jeremiah reads: 'Thou art my battle axe and weapons of war: for with thee will I break in pieces the nations, and with thee will I destroy kingdoms.' See *EL*, p. 104, for a description of the long genesis of the poem.

LATE LYRICS AND EARLIER (pp. 153–74)

First published 23 May 1922; manuscript in the Dorset County Museum.

p. 155 'Faintheart in a Railway Train': originally published as 'A Glimpse from the Train'.

p. 156 'A Man Was Drawing Near to Me': see *EL*, p. 92, in which Emma is quoted, remembering Hardy's first visit to Cornwall in March 1870. The places named in the poem are between St Juliot and the railway station at Launceston.

p. 159 'The Fallow Deer at the Lonely House': see Edward Thomas's poem 'Out in the Dark', a possible source.

p. 161 'On the Tune Called the Old-Hundred-and-Fourth': Ravenscroft's *Whole Book of Psalms* was published in 1621.

p. 162 'Voices from Things Growing in a Churchyard': the 'voices' in the poem are all members of Hardy's familys buried in Stinsford churchyard. **withwind**: clematis.

p. 164 'A Two-Years' Idyll': see also 'Overlooking the River Stour'.

p. 173 'Surview': the motto is from Psalm 69, verse 59: 'I thought on my ways'.

First published 20 November 1925; manuscript in the Library of Yale University.

p. 177 'Waiting Both': ll. 7–8, see Job 14:14.

p. 178 'Green Slates': Penpethy is near St Juliot in Cornwall. Hardy and Emma went there in 1870, to inspect slates for St Juliot church.

p. 179 'At Rushy-Pond': the pond is on the heath near Hardy's birthplace in Higher Bockhampton.

p. 181 'Snow in the Suburbs': Hardy and Emma lived for a short time in Surbiton after their marriage.

p. 182 'The Frozen Greenhouse': a further memory of Hardy's first visit to St Juliot in 1870.

p. 184 'Last Love-Word': Purdy associates this with Hardy's friend Mrs Henniker.

p. 184 'Nobody Comes': the poem refers to a time when Florence Hardy was briefly away from Max Gate, in hospital undergoing surgery.

p. 189 'On the Portrait of a Woman about to be Hanged': Mrs Edith Thompson, who murdered her husband, was hanged in Holloway Prison on 9 January 1923.

p. 190 'Once at Swanage': see also *EL*, p. 142.

p. 190 'Under High-Stoy Hill': High-Stoy Hill is ten miles north of Dorchester, on the road to Sherborne.

p. 192 'Retty's Phases': the manuscript draft of this poem is the earliest surviving draft of any poem by Hardy, dated 22 June 1868.

First published 2 October 1928, ten months after Hardy's death on 11 January 1928; manuscript in the Library of The Queen's College, Oxford. Hardy himself had prepared the volume for the press.

p. 202 'To Louisa in the Lane': see *EL*, pp. 33–4, for a reference to Hardy's youthful affection for Louisa Harding.

p. 205 'I Watched a Blackbird': H quotes a typescript of *LY* in the Dorset County Museum: 'April 15 [1900]. Easter Sunday. Watched a blackbird on a budding sycamore. Was near enough to see his tongue, and crocus-coloured bill parting and closing as he sang. He flew down; picked up a stem of hay, and flew up to where he was building.'

p. 207 'The Mongrel': Havenpool: Poole.

p. 211 'Standing by the Mantelpiece': H.M.M. is Horace Mosley Moule, Hardy's friend, who killed himself in Cambridge on 24 September 1873. See also 'Before My Friend Arrived'.

p. 217 'Dead "Wessex" the Dog to the Household: Wessex, Hardy's notorious dog, died 27 December 1926.

p. 220 'He Resolves to Say No More': H notes annotations to the manuscript: l. 1 '(One line from Agathias, Greek epigrammatist.) ["O my heart, leave the rest unknown." Mackail's trans. 218]'; l. 4 'Rev. VI. 8'; l. 18 recalls John 8:32: 'And ye shall know the truth, and the truth shall make you free.'

UNCOLLECTED POEMS (pp. 221–27)

p. 223 'Domicilium': an edition of the poem privately printed for Florence Hardy in 1918 says: 'The following lines, entitled "Domicilium", are the earliest known poem by Mr Thomas Hardy. It was written somewhere between the years 1857 and 1860, while he was still living with his parents at the charming cottage described in the verses, the birthplace of both himself and his father. The influence of Wordsworth, a favourite author of the youthful poet's, will be clearly perceived, also a strong feeling for the unique and desolate beauty of the adjoining heath.'

p. 224 'On the Doorstep': first published in the *Fortnightly Review* (April 1911) as number ten in the sequence 'Satires of Circumstance in Twelve Scenes'.

p. 224 'The Night of Trafalgár': *The Dynasts*, Part I, Act V, scene vii. The setting is Budmouth (Weymouth).

p. 225 'Budmouth Dears': *The Dynasts*, Part III, Act II, scene i.

p. 226 'The Eve of Waterloo': *The Dynasts*, Part III, Act VI, scene viii.

APPENDIX

p. 234 **Apology from** *Late Lyrics and Earlier*: see *SCC*, pp. 288–9 for evidence of Hardy's doubt about the wisdom of publishing this 'cantankerous' essay.

p. 241 **Introductory note to** *Winter Words*: l. 2: Hardy left his birthday blank, intending to supply it when he corrected the proofs of the book, but died before he could do so.

HARDY AND HIS CRITICS

It is clear from the Introduction to this edition that, until the last quarter of the century or so, critical comment on Hardy's poetry has been less extensive and generally less impressive than discussion of his novels. It is also clear that when Hardy published his first collection, *Wessex Poems*, in 1898 when he was fifty-eight, he had hopes of leading a quieter life than his fiction had allowed. He was disappointed. As his biographer Michael Millgate says:

> Immediately after the volume appeared, he again became a controversial figure. For his first significant appearance as a poet he had drawn widely on the entire range of the verse he had written to that date, almost as if he were more concerned to expose the full compass of his work than to display it and himself in the most favourable light. The impression of idiosyncracy given by the volume was heightened by the inclusion of the drawings, some hauntingly effective, others relatively crude in both conception and execution (Millgate, p. 392).

Reviews were mixed. The *Saturday Review* was violently hostile, referring to 'this curious and wearisome volume, these many slovenly, slipshod, uncouth verses, stilted in sentiment, poorly conceived and worse wrought'; the *Atheneum* was cool, finding it 'difficult to say the proper word'; and Lionel Johnson in the *Outlook*, though regretting a lack of humour, called the collection 'arresting, strenuous, sometimes admirable' (see Millgate, p. 606).

As Millgate points out, by far the commonest response to *Wessex Poems* was puzzlement: why had Hardy suddenly changed direction? During the next thirty or so years of his life, in which he published a further seven substantial collections, this element of surprise faded. But while Hardy's position as the Grand Old Man of English letters became unassailable, and influential admirers like Leslie Stephen and Charles Algernon

Swinburne were replaced by equally influential younger ones such as T. E. Lawrence and Siegfried Sassoon, the public response to his poetry remained divided. When *Human Shows*, the last volume to appear in his lifetime, was published in 1925, praise for his skill and stamina was still being offset by complaints about his gloominess.

Whether praising or blaming, very few of Hardy's original reviewers looked at his poems at all closely: they merely reacted to his moods. Edward Thomas was an exception. His prose work is dotted with references to Hardy, and he reviewed several of Hardy's individual volumes, some of them twice. Here is part of a piece he published about *Time's Laughingstocks* in the *Daily Chronicle* on 7 December 1909:

> There are sonnets in this book, but so unlike sonnets in spirit that many will read them without observing that they have this form. Often it might be thought that he dresses 'his thoughts' in these 'noble and famous garments' in a mood of solemn mockery. That, whether its intention or not, is its effect. He laughs at the external beauty of verse by making it clothe a corpse, a withered old man, or a woman of faded youth. The utmost positive effect of the verse is to give brevity and solemnity. The poems do not materially differ from his stories except that they are shorter than anything he has done in prose, and that they gain a greater solemnity from their more uniform colouring, their greater simplicity and lack of explanations.
>
> Many of the poems are narrative. Even when called lyrical they suggest a chain of events. They are full of misunderstandings, forebodings, endings, questionings. These the subjects [sic], and they are the atmosphere of the book, from which there is no escape. Other poetry allows a great richness and diversity of interpretation; Mr Hardy's allows none. He will not give his readers a moment's liberty. He gives them not only actions and characters, but their results; not only their results, but what is to be thought of them. He may not give us these things in so many words, but, if not, he does so by unmistakeable implication. We cannot think of any other poetry so tyrannous; and this in part makes us restive under the conventional form, which adds a grotesqueness by means of the necessary inversion and other poetic licence to the philosophic prose diction . . .
>
> The book contains ninety-nine reasons for not living. Yet it is not a book of despair. It is a book of sincerity, 'sweet sincerity', and to a poem of that name there is a memorable conclusion. It is dated 1899:

– Yet, would men look at true things,
And unilluded view things,
And count to bear undue things,

The real might mend the seeming,
Facts better their foredeeming,
And Life its disesteeming.

He does not believe that life is worth living as these men and
women lived, even if they did, and he gives us little chance of
believing so. But he thinks it is to be altered. He has a poem on a
christening, where a lovely mother makes the congregation smile
with pleasure – while the unmarried mother weeps on the gallery
stair:

'I am the baby's mother;
This gem of the race
The decent fain would smother,
And for my deep disgrace
I am bidden to leave the place.'

Bitter as the poem is there is hope in it. For it demands, at least,
if it does not foresee, a time when values and judgements will be
truer than they are, when we of our day shall be held as callous as
those who hung men for sheep-stealing. Mr Hardy looks at things
as they are, and what is still more notable he does not adopt the
genial consolation that they might be worse, that in spite of them
many are happy, and that the unhappy live on and will not die.
His worst tragedies are due as much to transient and alterable
custom as to the nature of things. He sees this, and he makes us
see it. The moan of his verse rouses an echo that is brave as a
trumpet.

Other poets, writing after Thomas, have also spoken up for
Hardy at times when critics have been indifferent or condescend-
ing. Edmund Blunden, for instance, in his study published in
1940, or W. H. Auden, who wrote in that same year: 'What I
valued most in Hardy [as a young writer], as I still do, was his
hawk's vision, his way of looking at life from a very great
height' (Southern Review, no. vi, 1940). Less than a decade
later, Philip Larkin was learning to appreciate Hardy for more
intimate and therefore, in a sense, for opposite reasons. In the
Introduction to the reissue of The North Ship (originally
published 1946, reissued 1966), Larkin remembers his early
obsession with Yeats, then says:

When reaction came, it was undramatic, complete and permanent. In early 1946 I had some new digs in which the bedroom faced east, so that the sun woke me inconveniently early. I used to read. One book I had at my bedside was the little blue *Chosen Poems of Thomas Hardy*: Hardy I knew as a novelist, but as regards his verse I shared Lytton Strachey's verdict that 'the gloom is not even relieved by a little elegance of diction'. This opinion did not last long; if I were asked to date its disappearance, I should guess it was the morning I first read 'Thoughts of Phena At News of Her Death'. Many years later, Vernon Watkins surprised me by saying that Dylan Thomas had admired Hardy above all poets of this century. 'He thought Yeats was the greatest by miles', he said. 'But Hardy was his favourite' (*Required Writing*, p. 223).

When Larkin himself was on the way to becoming a literary Grand Old Man, he developed his personal admiration for Hardy's poems into a plea for them to be shown general respect. It was not long in coming – but while Larkin deserves credit for this, the change in Hardy's poetic fortunes was further intensified by a broad shift in poetic taste during the third quarter of the century – a shift which Larkin also had a great deal to do with, and which sought to restore dignity to the native 'English line' while continuing to acknowledge the achievements of the Modernists.

James Granville Southworth, in *The Poetry of Thomas Hardy* (Colombia, 1947), anticipated many of Larkin's points and implications. Donald Davie wielded a broader, heavier sword in *Thomas Hardy and British Poetry* (London, 1973). His book, he said, was written 'so as to illustrate a thesis: that in British poetry of the last fifty years (as not in American) the most far-reaching influence, for good and ill, has been not Yeats, still less Eliot or Pound, but *Hardy*' (p. 3).

As Larkin was writing his articles in the 1960s, and while Davie was preparing his attack in the early 1970s, a handful of other critics made more methodical appraisals. Irving Howe, for instance, included a single chapter on Hardy's poems in his *Thomas Hardy* (London, 1968), in which he admitted to finding their 'sheer quantity ... discouraging', before insisting on Hardy's 'strange greatness', his 'splendid patience' and his 'tender caring for and affinity with his subjects' (pp. 160–67). A year later, Kenneth Marsden made an even more sober approach in *The Poems of Thomas Hardy: A Critical Introduc-*

tion (London, 1969), citing the testimony of John Davenport, C. Day Lewis, Robert Graves, Geoffrey Grigson, Ezra Pound and Dylan Thomas to prove Hardy's value, wondering about the preferences of 'Dr Leavis' and 'Dr Samuel Hynes' (who had published *The Pattern of Hardy's Poetry* in 1961), then suggesting that 'Much of [his] work exists at rather low tension and there are few "knock out" successes' (p. 8)). In the remainder of his book, Marsden rarely ventures from the shade of other critics to show us clearly what he thinks himself, but in his conclusion we can at least see what he agrees with:

> Ultimately, however, the reader who is trying to enjoy what Hardy has to offer will have to make the effort which has been suggested several times in this study, to see the poems as the poetic unity that many of them are, to be in contact with the poetic persona revealed here. If Hardy seems a little tentative, clumsy or indiscriminate, they should remember the remark of Joubert: 'Those who have no thoughts beyond their words, and no vision beyond their thoughts, have a very decisive style'; and also that of R. P. Blackmur about Hardy's personal rhythm: 'Once it has been struck out in the open, it is felt as ever present, not alone in his thirty or forty finest poems but almost everywhere in his work' (p. 223).

During the next decade, Hardy's critics became more robust. Even those like Jean Brooks, who continued to concentrate on Hardy's novels, allowed that his shaping genius was his poetic imagination. She wrote: 'The poetic relation to environment of these ephemeral creatures living and suffering in a remote part of Wessex lifts their story onto the cosmic plane of archetypal conflict of great ultimates' (*Thomas Hardy: The Poetic Structure*, London, 1973, p. 176). Others, writing about the poems only, developed this theme. The American poet James Richardson has interesting things to say about Hardy's relation to the Romantics and to Browning (*Thomas Hardy: The Poetry of Necessity*, Chicago, 1977). The poet Tom Paulin places Hardy in his Victorian context, discusses the ways in which he is 'both human, like a Dutch painting, and visionary' (p. 11), and – as his title, *Thomas Hardy: The Poetry of Perception* (London, 1977), suggests – explores the characteristics and effects of his 'perception'. He is especially good on the poem 'During Wind and Rain':

There is only what Hume would call a 'constant conjunction' between these objects [in the poem] which, indoors, gives them the appearance of being connected with each other. But they're really related only by familiarity or 'custom' which, for Hume, is just 'the effect of repeated perceptions'. Place some furniture on a lawn or a pair of spectacles on a field and the effect is disconcerting because their relationship appears unfamiliar and anomalous. Just as in 'I Travel Like a Phantom Now' man's consciousness is God's 'mistake', so his perception of the world is a casual anomaly that leaves no trace on the objects it registers. The values he brings to those objects don't belong to them. In Hume's terms all we know are the 'impressions' that things make on our senses, and so the 'poetry', the significance, of Hardy's eweleaze lies in his mind, not in the scene itself. The grey, cold, dispassionate illustration adds to the poem's theme – the impossibility of retrieving love – the indifference of the external world to both human emotions and the fact of its perception. It extends the poem's sense of the split in personal experience between past and present to include the anomalous relationship of man to the outer world which is the object of his knowledge. And the fact that their relationship is over and can never be renewed is mirrored in the total lack of relation between object and perceiver which the illustration expresses. There is no sense, as there is in Wordsworth and Coleridge, of a creative relationship between mind and fact' (p. 25).

Throughout the 1970s and 1980s, critical studies of Hardy's poems proliferated on both sides of the Atlantic – the most useful being John Bayley's *An Essay on Hardy* (Cambridge, 1978), J. O. Bailey's *The Poems of Thomas Hardy* (Chapel Hill, 1970) Philip Zeitler's *Moments of Vision* (Harvard, 1974), and William E. Buckler's *The Poetry of Thomas Hardy: A Study in Art and Ideas* (New York, 1983), which speaks sensibly about the 'sense of self' in Hardy's autobiography, and in a more convoluted way about the 'critical center' of his work:

A representative search of the records of the human consciousness for various meaningful clues to how the loss of man's paradise occurred and to how, in vicarious ways, it might be recovered is the critical center of Hardy's poetry. The moods, like the meters and the myths, are many, and true to the aesthetic genius with which he created them, Hardy let them remain 'fugitive', never attempting to imprison them in the 'harmonious philosophy' that would have greatly diminished their poetic integrity and imaginative truth. The speaker in the very first poem in his very first volume, 'The Temporary the All', identifies one of the chief ways in which people erode such happiness as 'Fate or [their] hand's achievement' brings their way – restless expectation of a more perfect tomorrow – and this maintains a persistent presence in the canon. The speaker in the last poem of the last (posthumous) volume, 'He Resolves to Say No More', decides to 'let all be,/And show to no man what I see' in recognition that, for better or worse, he has shown as much as saying can show of the past and that is 'blinkered sight' cannot expect to read the future. Between these two poles, Hardy's poetry-of-the-possible explores the various ways in which people 'ply spasmodically' their 'pleasuring' and their pain (p. 288).

Although they might be more sophisticated, and more convinced of their subject's merits, modern critical responses to Hardy's poems are still strikingly preoccupied with the aspects which concerned his earliest commentators: his pessimism, and the relationship between his self and the scene he contemplates. It is not surprising, then, that the most persuasive discussions of his poems are those which have come at them from a startling angle – a prickly, disapproving biographical angle in Robert Gittings's two-volume biography (London, 1975 and 1978), or an elaborately scholarly angle in Dennis Taylor's *Hardy's Literary Language and Victorian Philology* (Oxford, 1988). The latter is a fastidious, fascinating book; as it explains currently-neglected aspects of poetic form it shows the full extent of Hardy's technical genius. Hardy's career, Taylor reminds us, ran from the late 1850s to 1928. 'This time-span', he says, 'represents the climax and end of the 500-year era of accentual syllabic verse in English.' He ends by answering two questions which sound dull but in fact allow us to hear Hardy's true voice. He illuminates the Victorians' attitude to metrical form generally, and demonstrates Hardy's almost limitless technical ingenuity.

SUGGESTIONS FOR FURTHER READING

POEMS

Thomas Hardy: The Complete Poems, ed. James Gibson (London, 1976, reissued with corrections, 1978)

The Variorum Complete Poems of Thomas Hardy, ed. James Gibson (London, 1979)

The Complete Poetical Works of Thomas Hardy, Volume I, ed. Samuel Hynes (Oxford, 1982 *et seq.*)

LETTERS AND NOTEBOOKS

Selected Letters of Thomas Hardy, ed. Michael Millgate (Oxford, 1990)

The Personal Notebooks of Thomas Hardy, ed. R. H. Taylor (London, 1978)

BIBLIOGRAPHY

Richard Little Purdy, *Thomas Hardy: A Bibliographical Study* (Oxford, 1954, reissued 1978)

J. O. Bailey, *The Poems of Thomas Hardy, A Handbook and a Commentary* (Chapel Hill, 1970)

F. B. Pinion, *A Commentary on the Poems of Thomas Hardy* (London, 1976)

BIOGRAPHY

Florence Emily Hardy, *The Life of Thomas Hardy* (originally two volumes, London, 1928 and 1930; one volume 1962; ed. Michael Millgate and published as *The Life and Work of Thomas Hardy by Thomas Hardy*, Oxford, 1985)

Robert Gittings, *Young Thomas Hardy* (London, 1975) and *The Older Hardy* (London, 1978)

Michael Millgate, *Thomas Hardy: A Biography* (London, 1982)

Michael Seymour-Smith, *Hardy* (London, 1994)

BOOKS ABOUT HARDY'S POETRY

W. E. Buckler, *The Poetry of Thomas Hardy* (New York, 1983)

J. Cullen Brown, *A Journey into Hardy's Poetry* (London, 1989)

Donald Davie, *Thomas Hardy and British Poetry* (London, 1973)

James Gibson and T. Johnson (eds), *Thomas Hardy: Poems* (London, 1979)

Samuel Hynes, *The Pattern of Hardy's Poetry* (Chapel Hill, 1961)

Trevor Johnson, *A Critical Introduction to the Poems of Thomas Hardy* (London, 1991)

Tom Paulin, *Thomas Hardy: The Poetry of Perception* (London, 1977)

James Granville Southworth, *The Poetry of Thomas Hardy* (Colombia, 1947)

Dennis Taylor, *Hardy's Literary Language and Victorian Philology* (Oxford, 1988)

GENERAL BOOKS ABOUT HARDY

John Bayley, *An Essay on Hardy* (Cambridge, 1978)

Edmund Blunden, *Thomas Hardy* (London, 1940)

Louis Deacon and Terry Coleman, *Providence and Mr Hardy* (London, 1966)

Harold Orel, *Hardy: The Final Years* (London, 1976)

Norman Page, *Thomas Hardy* (London, 1977)

F. B. Pinion, *Thomas Hardy: Art and Thought* (London, 1971)

F. B. Pinion, *A Thomas Hardy Dictionary* (London, 1992)

ESSAYS, ARTICLES ETC. ABOUT HARDY'S POETRY

W. H. Auden, 'Hardy, A Literary Transference', *Southern Review* (no. vi, 1940)

R. G. Cox (ed.), *The Critical Heritage* (London, 1970)

Donald Davie, 'Hardy's Virgilian Purples', *Agenda* (Thomas Hardy Special Issue, vol. 8, 1972)

T. S. Eliot, 'Thomas Hardy', *After Strange Gods* (London, 1934)

Samuel Hynes, 'The Hardy Tradition in Modern English Poetry', *The Thomas Hardy Journal*, ed. James Gibson (October, 1986)

Philip Larkin, 'Mrs Hardy's Memories', 'Wanted: Good Hardy Critic', and 'The Poetry of Hardy', *Required Writing* (London, 1983)

F. R. Leavis, 'Hardy the Poet', *Southern Review* (no. vi, 1940)

F. R. Leavis, *New Bearings in English Poetry* (London, 1932)

Edward Thomas, *In Pursuit of Spring* (London, 1914)

INDEX OF FIRST LINES

INDEX OF TITLES

POETRY
IN EVERYMAN

Amorous Rites: Elizabethan Erotic Verse
edited by Sandra Clark
Erotic and often comic poems dealing with myths of transformation and erotic interaction between humans and gods
£4.99

Selected Poems
JOHN KEATS
An excellent selection of the poetry of one of the principal figures of the Romantic movement
£6.99

Poems and Prose
CHRISTINA ROSSETTI
A new collection of her writings, poetry and prose, marking the centenary of her death
£5.99

Poems and Prose
P. B. SHELLEY
The essential Shelley in one volume
£5.99

Silver Poets of the Sixteenth Century
edited by Douglas Brooks-Davies
An exciting and comprehensive collection
£6.99

Complete English Poems
JOHN DONNE
The father of metaphysical verse in this highly-acclaimed collection
£6.99

Complete English Poems, Of Education, Areopagitica
JOHN MILTON
An excellent introduction to Milton's poetry and prose
£6.99

Women Romantic Poets 1780–1830: An Anthology
edited by Jennifer Breen
Hidden talent from the Romantic era rediscovered
£5.99

Selected Poems
D. H. LAWRENCE
An authoritative selection spanning the whole of Lawrence's literary career
£4.99

The Poems
W. B. YEATS
Ireland's greatest lyric poet surveyed in this ground-breaking edition
£7.99

All books are available from your local bookshop or direct from:
Littlehampton Book Services Cash Sales, 14 Eldon Way, Lineside Estate,
Littlehampton, West Sussex BN17 7HE *(prices are subject to change)*

To order any of the books, please enclose a cheque (in sterling) made payable to
Littlehampton Book Services, or phone your order through with credit card details (Access,
Visa or Mastercard) on 01903 721596 (24 hour answering service) stating card number
and expiry date. *(Please add £1.25 for package and postage to the total of your order.)*

In the USA, for further information and a complete catalogue call 1-800-526-2778

CLASSIC NOVELS
IN EVERYMAN

The Time Machine
H. G. WELLS
*One of the books which defined
'science fiction' – a compelling
and tragic story of a brilliant
and driven scientist*
£3.99

Oliver Twist
CHARLES DICKENS
*Arguably the best-loved of
Dickens's novels. With all the
original illustrations*
£4.99

Barchester Towers
ANTHONY TROLLOPE
*The second of Trollope's
Chronicles of Barsetshire,
and one of the funniest of all
Victorian novels*
£4.99

The Heart of Darkness
JOSEPH CONRAD
*Conrad's most intense, subtle,
compressed, profound and
proleptic work*
£3.99

Tess of the d'Urbervilles
THOMAS HARDY
*The powerful, poetic classic
of wronged innocence*
£3.99

Wuthering Heights and Poems
EMILY BRONTË
*A powerful work of genius – one of
the great masterpieces of literature*
£3.99

Pride and Prejudice
JANE AUSTEN
*Proposals, rejections, infidelities,
elopements, happy marriages –
Jane Austen's most popular novel*
£2.99

North and South
ELIZABETH GASKELL
*A novel of hardship, passion
and hard-won wisdom amidst the
conflicts of the industrial revolution*
£4.99

The Newcomes
W. M. THACKERAY
*An exposé of Victorian polite
society by one of the nineteenth-
century's finest novelists*
£6.99

Adam Bede
GEORGE ELIOT
*A passionate rural drama enacted
at the turn of the eighteenth
century*
£5.99

All books are available from your local bookshop or direct from:
Littlehampton Book Services Cash Sales, 14 Eldon Way, Lineside Estate,
Littlehampton, West Sussex BN17 7HE (*prices are subject to change*)

To order any of the books, please enclose a cheque (in sterling) made payable to
Littlehampton Book Services, or phone your order through with credit card details (Access,
Visa or Mastercard) on 01903 721596 (24 hour answering service) stating card number
and expiry date. (*Please add £1.25 for package and postage to the total of your order.*)

In the USA, for further information and a complete catalogue call 1-800-526-2778

CLASSIC FICTION
IN EVERYMAN

**The Impressions of
Theophrastus Such**
GEORGE ELIOT
*An amusing collection of character
sketches, and the only paperback
edition available*
£5.99

Frankenstein
MARY SHELLEY
*A masterpiece of Gothic terror in
its original 1818 version*
£3.99

East Lynne
MRS HENRY WOOD
*A classic tale of melodrama,
murder and mystery*
£7.99

**Holiday Romance and
Other Writings for Children**
CHARLES DICKENS
*Dickens's works for children,
including 'The Life of Our Lord'
and 'A Child's History of England',
with original illustrations*
£5.99

The Ebb-Tide
R.L. STEVENSON
*A compelling study of ordinary
people in extreme circumstances*
£4.99

The Three Impostors
ARTHUR MACHEN
*The only edition available
of this cult thriller*
£4.99

Mister Johnson
JOYCE CARY
*The only edition available of this
amusing but disturbing twentieth-
century tale*
£5.99

The Jungle Book
RUDYARD KIPLING
*The classic adventures of Mowgli
and his friends*
£3.99

Glenarvon
LADY CAROLINE LAMB
*The only edition available of the
novel which throws light on the
greatest scandal of the early nine-
teenth century – the infatuation of
Caroline Lamb with Lord Byron*
£6.99

**Twenty Thousand Leagues
Under the Sea**
JULES VERNE
*Scientific fact combines with
fantasy in this prophetic tale
of underwater adventure*
£4.99

All books are available from your local bookshop or direct from:
Littlehampton Book Services Cash Sales, 14 Eldon Way, Lineside Estate,
Littlehampton, West Sussex BN17 7HE (*prices are subject to change*)

To order any of the books, please enclose a cheque (in sterling) made payable to
Littlehampton Book Services, or phone your order through with credit card details (Access,
Visa or Mastercard) on 01903 721596 (24 hour answering service) stating card number
and expiry date. (*Please add £1.25 for package and postage to the total of your order.*)

In the USA, for further information and a complete catalogue call 1-800-526-2778

SHORT STORY COLLECTIONS
IN EVERYMAN

The Strange Case of Dr Jekyll and Mr Hyde and Other Stories
R. L. STEVENSON
An exciting selection of gripping tales from a master of suspense
£1.99

Nineteenth-Century American Short Stories
edited by Christopher Bigsby
A selection of the works of Henry James, Edith Wharton, Mark Twain and many other great American writers
£6.99

The Best of Saki
edited by MARTIN STEPHEN
Includes Tobermory, Gabriel Ernest, Svedni Vashtar, The Interlopers, Birds on the Western Front
£4.99

Souls Belated and Other Stories
EDITH WHARTON
Brief, neatly crafted tales exploring a range of themes from big taboo subjects to the subtlest little ironies of social life
£6.99

The Night of the Iguana and Other Stories
TENNESSEE WILLIAMS
Twelve remarkable short stories, each a compelling drama in miniature
£4.99

Selected Short Stories and Poems
THOMAS HARDY
Hardy's most memorable stories and poetry in one volume
£4.99

Selected Tales
HENRY JAMES
Stories portraying the tensions between private life and the outside world
£5.99

The Best of Sherlock Homes
ARTHUR CONAN DOYLE
All the favourite adventures in one volume
£4.99

The Secret Self 1: *Short Stories by Women*
edited by Hermione Lee
'*A superb collection*' The Guardian
£4.99

All books are available from your local bookshop or direct from:
Littlehampton Book Services Cash Sales, 14 Eldon Way, Lineside Estate,
Littlehampton, West Sussex BN17 7HE (*prices are subject to change*)

To order any of the books, please enclose a cheque (in sterling) made payable to
Littlehampton Book Services, or phone your order through with credit card details (Access,
Visa or Mastercard) on 01903 721596 (24 hour answering service) stating card number
and expiry date. (*Please add £1.25 for package and postage to the total of your order.*)

In the USA, for further information and a complete catalogue call 1-800-526-2778

WOMEN'S WRITING
IN EVERYMAN

Poems and Prose
CHRISTINA ROSSETTI
*A collection of her writings, poetry
and prose, published to mark the
centenary of her death*
£5.99

Women Philosophers
edited by Mary Warnock
*The great subjects of philosophy
handled by women spanning four
centuries, including Simone de
Beauvoir and Iris Murdoch*
£6.99

Glenarvon
LADY CAROLINE LAMB
*A novel which throws light on the
greatest scandal of the early nine-
teenth century – the infatuation of
Caroline Lamb with Lord Byron*
£6.99

Women Romantic Poets
1780 – 1830: **An Anthology**
edited by Jennifer Breen
*Hidden talent from the Romantic
era rediscovered*
£5.99

**Memoirs of the Life of Colonel
Hutchinson**
LUCY HUTCHINSON
*One of the earliest pieces of
women's biographical writing, of
great historic and feminist interest*
£6.99

**The Secret Self 1: Short Stories
by Women**
edited by Hermione Lee
'A superb collection' The Guardian
£4.99

The Age of Innocence
EDITH WHARTON
*A tale of the conflict between love
and tradition by one of America's
finest women novelists*
£4.99

Frankenstein
MARY SHELLEY
*A masterpiece of Gothic terror
in its original 1818 version*
£3.99

The Life of Charlotte Brontë
ELIZABETH GASKELL
*A moving and perceptive tribute
by one writer to another*
£4.99

Victorian Women Poets
1830 – 1900
edited by Jennifer Breen
*A superb anthology of the era's
finest female poets*
£5.99

**Female Playwrights of the
Restoration: Five Comedies**
edited by Paddy Lyons
*Rediscovered literary treasure
in a unique selection*
£5.99

All books are available from your local bookshop or direct from:
Littlehampton Book Services Cash Sales, 14 Eldon Way, Lineside Estate,
Littlehampton, West Sussex BN17 7HE (*prices are subject to change*)

To order any of the books, please enclose a cheque (in sterling) made payable to
Littlehampton Book Services, or phone your order through with credit card details (Access,
Visa or Mastercard) on 01903 721596 (24 hour answering service) stating card number
and expiry date. (*Please add £1.25 for package and postage to the total of your order.*)

In the USA, for further information and a complete catalogue call 1-800-526-2778